ASPIRE
SUCCEED
PROGRESS

Cambridge Lower Secondary

Complete English

Series Editor: Dean Roberts
Alan Jenkins, Mark Pedroz,
Jane Arredondo, Annabel Charles,
Tony Parkinson

Second Edition

WORKBOOK

OXFORD
UNIVERSITY PRESS

Great Clarendon Street, Oxford, OX2 6DP, United Kingdom

Oxford University Press is a department of the University of Oxford.

It furthers the University's objective of excellence in research, scholarship, and education by publishing worldwide. Oxford is a registered trade mark of Oxford University Press in the UK and in certain other countries

British Library Cataloguing in Publication Data
Data available

978-1-38-201949-1

10 9 8 7 6 5 4 3 2

Paper used in the production of this book is a natural, recyclable product made from wood grown in sustainable forests.

The manufacturing process conforms to the environmental regulations of the country of origin.

Printed in China by Golden Cup

Acknowledgements

The publisher and authors would like to thank the following for permission to use photographs and other copyright material:

Cover: Beastfromeast/Getty Images

Photos: p31: Lemberg Vector studio / Shutterstock; **p69(l):** Artefact / Alamy Stock Photo; **p69(r):** The Picture Art Collection / Alamy Stock Photo.

Artwork by Six Red Marbles, Q2A Media, and Oxford University Press.

Franz Kafka: Metamorphosis from The Metamorphosis and Other Stories translated by Joyce Crick (Oxford World Classics, 2009), translation copyright © Joyce Crick 2009, Oxford University Press. Reproduced with permission of the Licensor through PLSclear.

Jane Asher: Eats for Treats (BBC Books, 1990), reprinted by permission of the author c/o Furniss Lawton, James Grant Group, London.

Malala Yousafzai: speech to the United Nations, July 2013, copyright © Malala Yousafzai 2013, Curtis Brown Book Group Ltd, London.

Eva Ibbotson: Journey to the River Sea (Macmillan, 2011), reprinted by permission of Macmillan Children's Books, London, UK.

Gerald Durrell: My Family and Other Animals (Penguin, 1959), copyright © Gerald Durrell 1956, Curtis Brown Book Group Ltd, London, on behalf of the Beneficiaries of the Estate of Gerald Durrell.

Orhan Pamuk: Snow translated by Maureen Freely (Faber, 2010), translation copyright © 2004 by Alfred A Knop, a division of Penguin Random House LLC, copyright © Orham Pamuk 2003, reprinted by permission of the Wylie Agency (UK) Ltd and Alfred A Knopf, an imprint of Knopf Doubleday Publishing Group, a division of Penguin Random House LLC. All rights reserved.

Every effort has been made to contact copyright holders of material reproduced in this book. Any omissions will be rectified in subsequent printings if notice is given to the publisher.

Table of contents

Narrative viewpoints

Fiction genres

Look at the types of books here and draw lines to match them with the opening sentences from the first chapters.

Fantasy

Children's

Young adult

Murder mystery

Romance

Sci-fi

Adventure

a Arthur the aardvark eats ants.

b Pino's sister could never remember anything. But she remembered that she had seen him passing a note to Amelia and, when she got in from school, she told his mother.

c It was a bright, silver-cold frosty night. Elliot looked out of his window, waiting for the signal. He waited and waited, and then it came. A puff of what could only be smoke, from what could only be a curiously small dragon.

d 'Solving mysteries, eh?' the colonel laughed. 'You won't find many mysteries in this house, or any murders, I can tell you that.'

'Oh, but I already have,' replied Miss Teaparty. 'There's a dead body inside your grandfather clock.'

e Silvia leaned against the arm of her beau and sighed. They were so happy together now, but it hadn't always been like that. She let her mind drift back to the first time she had met Olivier . . .

f The steel tube that was their transport and home was out of control. Quggy looked at the Oglo sitting at the control panel and wondered. *Was he loyal to the Mother Ship or was he deliberately taking them out of orbit?*

g Robin of Loxley threw back his hood. 'Don't be too sure of that,' he said, 'I have a dozen men with longbows outside.'

'You!' shouted the Sheriff. 'How did you get here?'

'Over the moat,' Robin shrugged.

'Guards!' screamed the Sheriff.

Metamorphosis

'What has happened to me?' he thought. It was not a dream. His room, a proper human being's room, rather too small, lay peacefully between its four familiar walls. (…)

Gregor's gaze then turned towards the window, and the murky weather—one could hear the raindrops striking the window-sill—made him quite melancholy. 'What if I went on sleeping for a while and forgot all these idiocies?', he thought, but that was quite impossible, as he was used to sleeping on his right side and in his present state he was unable to get himself into this position. However energetically he flung himself onto his right side, whenever he did so he would rock onto his back again. He must have tried a hundred times, shutting his eyes so that he didn't have to see his jittery legs, and he only gave over when he began to feel a slight ache in his side, something he had never felt before.

From *Metamorphosis* by Franz Kafka

Write out this scene from *Metamorphosis* in the first person as if you are Gregor. Try to keep the same atmosphere and the same actions, but try to imagine what Gregor is thinking and feeling as if it is happening to you.

....

....

....

....

....

....

....

....

....

....

....

Types of sentence

1. Match lines **a** to **e** below to these types of sentence. The first two are done for you.

Interrogative (question) ....<u>b</u>........   Simple ....

Imperative/Command (order) ....<u>a</u>........   Complex ....

Compound ....

a 'Jump!'

b 'Jump the fence?'

c 'She jumped over the fence.'

d He opened the gate and walked into the street.

e The boy, who was lazy and very unfit, opened the gate because it was easier than jumping over the fence.

2. Think of three more single word verbs that can be used as imperatives or commands. For example: Stop!

....

3. A simple sentence contains only one clause. A compound sentence has two main clauses joined by a coordinating conjunction: *and, or, but*.

She opened the gate. (simple sentence)

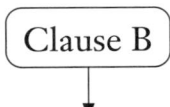

She opened the gate but did not shut it. (compound sentence)

Write this paragraph so it has simple and compound sentences. Add coordinating conjunctions and punctuation to make the compound sentences.

I don't like going to parties I especially don't like swimming pool parties my friends were going I wanted to be with my friends it was awful the music was too loud I got a headache I was sick on the way home I missed my bus

....

....

Gulliver's travels

In a little time, I felt something alive moving on my left leg, which advancing gently forward over my breast, came almost up to my chin; when bending mine eyes downwards as much as I could, I perceived it to be a human creature not six inches high, with a bow and arrow in his hands, and a quiver at his back. In the meantime, I felt at least forty more of the same kind (as I conjectured) following the first. I was in the utmost astonishment, and roared so loud, that they all ran back in a fright; and some of them, as I was afterward told, were hurt with the falls they got by leaping from my sides upon the ground. However, they soon returned, and one of them, who ventured so far as to get a full sight of my face, lifting up his hands and eyes by way of admiration, cried out in a shrill, but distinct voice, *Hekinah degul*.

From Gulliver's Travels by Jonathan Swift

The author Jonathan Swift wrote *Gulliver's Travels* in the first person as if he were Gulliver. Read this extract carefully and rewrite it in the third person as if you were one of the small people of Lilliput.

....

....

....

....

....

....

....

....

....

....

....

Complex sentences and clauses

A complex sentence has a main clause and one or more subordinate or dependent clauses. The main clause is the most important part of the sentence. The term *complex* describes the grammatical structure; it doesn't mean it has to be a long or difficult sentence. Look at these short complex sentences.

I admit that I have made a mistake.

They told everyone the good news that they had passed the exam.

1. The best way to see how simple and complex sentences work is to change them around. Make each of these pairs of simple sentences into one complex sentence.

   The first one is done for you.

   a I was gazing out of the window. I saw a strange sort of cat.

   As I was gazing out of the window I saw a strange cat. *Or*

   I saw a strange cat while I was gazing out of the window.

   b She found a book. She was on her way to the library.

   ....

   c He works hard at school. He wants to be a lawyer.

   ....

   d They heard beautiful music. They were passing a concert hall.

   ....

2. Underline the adverbs and adverbial phrases in the paragraph below that show where, when or how. The first one is done for you.

   Standing in the queue, we waited for the show to begin. While we were waiting, a street performer did a dance. As soon as the show began, I realised it hadn't been worth waiting for. Within a few minutes I was asleep; this often happens when I'm bored.

3. Write three sentences about your daily school routine using fronted adverbials. Start each sentence with a phrase that tells the reader when, where or how.

   Start like this: Every morning I get up at . . .

   ....

   ....

Writing a script

Here is an excerpt from the conversation between Josh and Melanie about fantasy movies.

Josh:	Since when does a fantasy story have to be realistic? That's silly. The whole thing about fantasy stories and movies is that they aren't realistic. And they are all different.
Melanie:	The basic stories are the same, though. Good versus evil. The hero everybody loves is in danger. Will he survive? Will he save the princess? All stories are basically the same. They are all about male heroes as well for that matter.
Josh:	Female heroes are called heroines.
Melanie:	(*laughing*) You won't win any arguments that way, Josh. What I'm saying is that the basic plot of most of these movies is more or less the same.

Write a similar dialogue in the form of a script between two friends who are discussing action movies.

- Keep the dialogue informal.
- Underline colloquial expressions that you would not use with anyone except your friends. There is no need to be too rude!

Here is an example:

Josh: I love Star Wars movies. <u>They're ace.</u>
Melanie: Star Wars! <u>What a load of rubbish.</u>

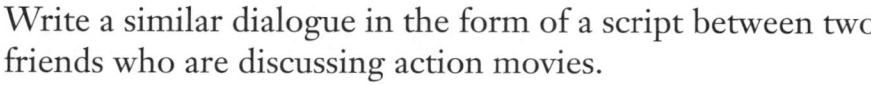

The narrator's voice

When you plan a story you need to decide who is telling it because this is who the reader hears when they are reading.

Read this extract and answer the questions.

> Fenner the dragon raised his head and sniffed, but he could smell nothing except his own foul odour in the closed, stale cave. Something had disturbed him from his winter-long sleep. He shifted his weight and pecked off a few bits of gold and silver, brooches and cloak clasps that had stuck to his soft underside then checked the domed ring was in its place. Slowly, stiff from so long in one position, he raised himself up off his nest and stretched each leg, arching his ridged back to ease his spine. He had grown even bigger and fatter over the winter despite so many weeks without food and his lair was now a very tight fit.
>
> His stomach rumbled: he was hungry and very thirsty.
>
> From *The Dragonslayer's Servant* by Jane Arrendondo

1. a Which type of narrator and from whose point of view does the writer describe the scene?

....

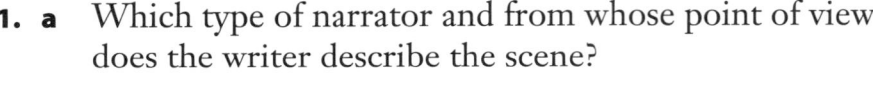

b Give a reason to support your answer.

....

....

2. Continue the story of Fenner the dragon in the first person, from Fenner's point of view.

....

....

....

....

....

....

Testing my skills

1. If a novel started with these lines, what fiction genre would you place it in?

> The door had clearly been purposely left open, and on the floor there were two sets of footprints. Carter and Todd had made up their minds. An inside job.

2. What narrative voice is being used here? Tick (✓) the correct answer.

> *You know you are guilty. You were there. These footprints are clear to see, and the shoes you are currently wearing look very similar indeed to those in the photograph.*

First person ☐
Second person ☐
Third person ☐

3. Which of these applies to the use of a semi-colon? Circle all that apply.

  A Used less often than a colon

  B Introduces a list

  C Joins closely connected ideas in a sentence

  D To work properly should link related or complementary ideas

4. What is this a definition of? Tick (✓) the correct answer.

> *The use of humour, irony, exaggeration or ridicule to expose and criticise people's stupidity or extreme views, particularly in the context of politics*

Irony ☐
The works of William Shakespeare ☐
Satire ☐
Hyperbole ☐

5. Fill in the gaps with suitable embedded or subordinate clauses.

    a I used to live in Transylvania ....

    b .... it all happened

    when I was a vampire.

    c I woke up one day .... and

    everything became better.

6. Here are some facts.

> - I am a film director.
> - My next film will be about a crime heist in Los Angeles.
> - Nobody dies.

    a Use these details to write a proposal to a Hollywood film company using a formal register.

    b Do the same again but using an informal register.

7. In your opinion, and with regard to characterisation only, why should a book always, or never, be made into a film? Fill in both.

    Always: ....

    ....

    Never: ....

    ....

8. Match these snippets from fiction books to the appropriate narrative voice.

I saw them and I spoke to them, and I gasped in wonderment.	Dialogue
You stayed up all night having fun; you cannot help us now as you are too tired.	Third person limited
Stay clear, we don't know who they are!	Second person narrative
It was clearly an alien race from another planet with bad intentions.	First person narrative
Maybe they were aliens; maybe they were gene-enhanced FBI agents. Who knows?	Third person omniscient

② Discovering the past

Discovering the past and finding the future

Answer the following questions.

1. Look at the list of occupations below. Find out what each person does for a living and write a brief description.

   The first one is done for you.

   a Palaeontologist: Palaeontologists study fossils. They take part in digs and study the remains of dinosaurs, plants and organisms to help us understand the distant past.

   b Biologist: ....

   ....

   ....

   c Geologist: ....

   ....

   ....

   d Zoologist: ....

   ....

   ....

   e Archaeologist: ....

   ....

   ....

2. Choose one of the occupations from the list and say why you might consider it for a career. If none of the occupations appeal to you, say why.

   ....

   ....

   ....

   ....

   ....

An interview with a palaeontologist

Write a short interview to be broadcast during a radio science programme. You are the interviewer and you are talking to a palaeontologist who has found a remarkable collection of very ancient bones buried in volcanic ash.

Write your interview in the form of a script. The beginning has been written for you.

Interviewer (I): _Good evening and welcome to 'Dramatic Discoveries', the programme about exploration and discovery. This evening I am talking to:_

(Interviewee's initials): ....

....

I: ....

Script for the main interview:

....

....

....

....

....

....

....

....

....

....

....

....

....

....

....

....

| | | Femur | Tibia |

Direct and reported speech – the discovery of Lucy

Sam and Maria are talking about the discovery of a skeleton named 'Lucy' in 1974.

Read their conversation, then write what Maria tells Sam as reported speech.

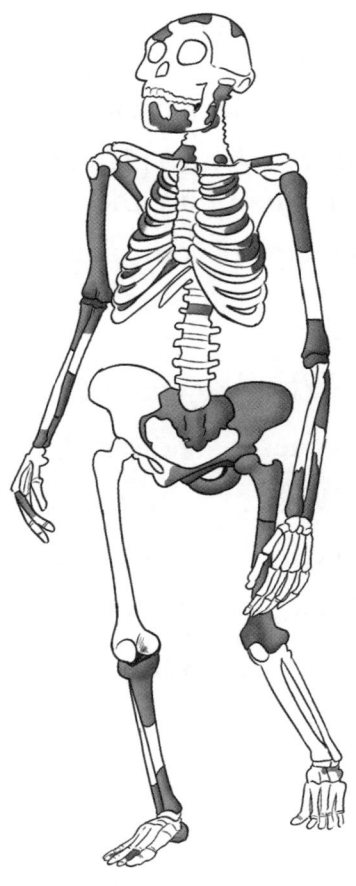

"So who or what was Lucy?" asked Sam.

"A member of Australopithecus afarensis," said Maria.

"How do we know that?" Sam demanded.

"Because Donald Johanson, a palaeoanthropologist, and his companion Tom Gray were looking for fossils at a lakeside site known to be 3.2 million years old in the Afar region of Ethiopia," Maria explained.

"What did they actually find?"

"First, an elbow bone. Then they found bits of skull, part of a jaw and vertebrae. In the end they uncovered about 40 percent of the skeleton. Up to now, I think it's the most complete early human ever discovered."

....

....

....

....

....

....

....

....

....

....

The start of a scary story

You are going to plan a paragraph that forms the opening scene for a scary story. It can be a traditional scary story or you can make it funny. It must have a nasty surprise though.

Make a 'Wh…' plan using some of the details below to help you. Do not use them all. You can invent details of your own.

Remember your plan is for an opening scene, not the whole story.

'Wh…' plan			
Where:	castle	pyramid	ancient battlefield
When:	at dusk	just before midnight	just before dawn
Who:	Dr True	Old Ebenezer	Selina Weathervane
What:	a rusty sword	an old wicker basket	digging tools (spade or trowel)

A spectacular discovery

1. You are an explorer in a dangerous place such as a cave, desert or mountain. You make a spectacular discovery. Write an account of what happens.

....

....

....

....

....

....

....

....

....

....

....

....

2. Underline all the prepositions and prepositional phrases you have used in your account.

3. Describe what you find. Since this is a unique discovery, make up portmanteau words or invent words of your own. Underline your portmanteau and invented words.

   Here is an example: Near the edge of the cliff I saw a very curious fossil. This thing, which I shall call a 'snakil', had the long shape of a serpent with a large shell like that of snail on its back . . .

....

....

....

....

....

King Richard III

A news reporter has written ten sentences about the discovery of the skeleton of Richard III, but the sentences are not in order.

1. Write numbers against the sentences to show the correct order. The first one has been done for you.

1 You may have heard of King Richard III.

When the archaeologists found the skeleton, they were hopeful it was Richard III because it had a crooked spine (from a condition called scoliosis).

He is the king in Shakespeare's play who is supposed to have murdered his nephews.

Richard ruled as king of England from 1483 to 1485.

The king was also rumoured to have a withered arm, but there was no evidence of that on the skeleton.

The car park is about 25 kilometres from the battlefield where the king was killed.

He died in battle aged 32 at a place called Bosworth Field near Leicester.

Archaeologists and members of the Richard III Society have been searching for the bones for years.

Historians now say they are studying sources to find out more about the real King Richard.

In September 2012 they finally found them – under a city car park.

2. Now write an informal news report based on your sentences.

New fabrics for sportswear

Read the following paragraph and summarise why modern microfibre fabrics make good sportswear.
Write 40–50 words.

Microfibre clothing is skin-friendly and does not contain allergy-producing substances. The open air channels in microfibres also mean there is healthy exchange of heat and moisture because they carry away sweat from the skin. Wearing cotton for a workout may seem sensible because we wear cotton in hot weather, but in a very short time you'll be wearing a tee-shirt drenched in body moisture. Then, as your core body temperature cools down, you run the risk of getting post-workout chills. Eventually, your cotton shirt will dry, but you'll be left feeling cold and clammy. Microfibre fabrics are water-repellent and, contrary to what many people think, they are 'naturally breathing' fibres, which is why they make excellent sports and leisurewear.

....

....

....

....

....

....

....

....

....

....

....

....

....

Testing my skills

1. If a writer stated: "The sharp-toothed beast looked as tall as a building", what literary technique is the writer using?

....

2. Look at these two examples, one of direct speech, the other of reported speech. Circle the most effective.

   a Direct speech:

   "It's huge, it's a colossus, it looks like a creature from another world," said Shania.

   b Reported speech:

   On seeing the colossal animal in front of her, Shania told her friend of its alien-like presence.

3. Using humour to make a character or speaker look foolish is a common device used by which of these? Circle those which apply.

   A Dramatists

   B Story writers

   C Poets

   D Satirists

4. Which of these is a portmanteau word/phrase? Circle **two** words/phrases.

   A blog

   B suitcase

   C news report

   D edutainment

5. Fill in the gaps with suitable prepositions.

   .... the haunted castle the ghost sat .... the curtain that fell .... the floor. When the new inhabitants arrived, the ghost arose and floated .... Very soon, there would be plenty .... amusement.

6. Which of these are key skills for summary writing?
   Circle those which apply.

   A Using your own words to link details together

   B Including at least two details per paragraph

   C Repeating some of the key words from the main text

   D Using strong discourse markers

   E Always trying to cover the points from a general
      perspective

7. The discovery of a long-lost city under the Pacific Ocean
   was reported on a history website. Give a suitable title for
   the report and provide a quick summary of the contents.
   (Hint – you can make up the details.)

   Title: ....

   Contents: ....

   ....

   ....

   ....

   ....

   ....

8. Note-making is a useful skill when reading longer extracts.
   Give two key points to always follow when making notes.

   ● ....

   ....

   ● ....

   ....

(3) Influencers

Qualities and personality traits

1. Use a thesaurus to find five unusual words to describe someone's appearance and five words for character or personality.

   a Appearance ....

   ....

   b Character ....

   ....

2. What personal qualities should the following people have?

   a A nurse ....

   b A fire-fighter ....

   c A teacher ....

   d A politician ....

   e A foreign correspondent for a TV news channel ....

   ....

   f A model ....

   g An engineer ....

3. Choose a career for yourself. It can be one of the professions above or something different. Write a paragraph outlining two or more reasons why you are suited to this type of work.

....

....

....

....

....

....

....

....

....

....

Famous forever

Everyone on this page is famous for being brave, beautiful or clever, or a combination of all three.

Draw lines to match each name to the reason why the person is famous.

1. She became queen of Egypt in 48 BCE and died after losing a war with the Romans.

2. He was the first European to sail to India in 1497. He sailed round the Cape of Good Hope and an Arab sailor showed him how to cross the Indian Ocean.

3. He was a Swedish chemist, engineer, inventor and philanthropist whose name is famous for international prizes.

4. She was famous for being married to a king and died during a revolution after telling people to eat cake.

5. He was born in 1829. He was the leader of the Chiricahua Apache Indians. He led his people in battle against white settlers. He was caught and sent to Florida in 1886.

6. He led the movement for independence against the British in India. He lived a very simple life without luxuries. He taught people to rebel without violence. He was assassinated in 1948.

7. He was a South African politician. He campaigned against white rule in South Africa, then asked people to forgive each other.

8. She was born in Poland in 1867. She was a Nobel Prize winner. She died as a result of carrying test tubes of radium in her pockets during research on mobile X-ray units.

9. He was a Chinese philosopher and teacher who lived between 551 and 479 BCE.

10. She is famous for her smile, and for the artist who painted her portrait between 1503 and 1507.

Tick the names of the people you recognise, and find out about the people you don't.

Confucius

Mona Lisa

Geronimo

Marie Curie

Alfred Nobel

Vasco da Gama

Cleopatra

Marie Antoinette

Nelson Mandela

Mahatma Gandhi

Adjectives to describe people

We often convert nouns to adjectives using the suffix *-able*.
We say someone who gives to a charity is *charitable*. Someone
we respect for their capability is *capable*.

1. Write in the missing words.

Nouns	Adjectives
charity	charitable
....	dependable
fashion	....
....	reliable

2. Choose two adjectives to describe people and use them
in sentences.

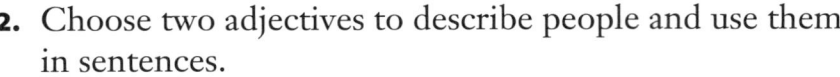

....

3. Some adjectives that come from nouns use the suffix *-ous*
or *-ious*. Fill in the gaps.

Nouns	Adjectives
mischief	mischievous
....	famous
prosperity	....
....	cautious
study	....
mystery	....

4. Write the nouns for the following adjectives. Use a
dictionary to help you.

   a Aggressive ....

   b Argumentative ....

   c Secretive ....

   d Manipulative ....

5. Put a tick beside the adjectives in tasks 3 and 4 that describe
positive characteristics and a cross beside those that are negative.

Case study

1. Find out about someone who lived or still lives in your area (town, county or province) who is either well-known or should be well-known. Say why this person deserves to be admired and/or respected.

2. Share your findings with your class: how many of you have chosen the same person, and why?

3. Use this grid to help you make notes from your research then write a paragraph about your chosen person.

Questions for investigation	Your comments
1. What is the subject's (person's) name?	
2. Why should this person be better known?	
3. What have they done or achieved?	
4. What qualities does this person have that you admire or respect?	

....

....

....

....

....

....

....

....

....

Tricky spellings

1. Make verbs from the following nouns.

a Advertisement ....

b Surprise ....

c Compromise ....

d Advice ....

e Practice ....

f Revision ....

g Amazement ....

h Television ....

i Organisation ....

j Sympathy ....

Verbs to adjectives

Some adjectives have the suffix -*able* and some use -*ible*, for example, cap*able* and horr*ible*.

2. Change the following verbs to adjectives.

a To notice ....

b To access ....

c To adapt ....

d To believe ....

e To reverse ....

f To collapse ....

g To rely ....

3. Finish the words in this paragraph.

It was a terr.................... morning. There was a horr....................

noise outside and I had an unbear .... headache.

My English teacher wasn't very symp.................... at first,

and critic.................... my spelling. She said my handwriting

was illeg...................., too. Then, to my sur...................., she

adv.................... me to drink a glass of water. I felt better

afterwards but then remembered I hadn't revi....................

for our maths test later.

Article on unsung heroes

There has been a terrible accident in your local area. Many people you know were in danger but got to safety thanks to the help of their neighbours or local residents, the police and the fire brigade.

You are a reporter for the local newspaper. Write a short article on what these people did and why you admire them.

You may use some or all of the following words and phrases in your letter.

| bravery | unselfish action | courageous | fearless |
| well-trained | skilful | generous | rapid response |

Start like this:

Unsung heroes!

Every day we hear the names of famous people but... ....

....

....

....

....

....

....

....

....

....

....

....

Famous mysteries

Read this summary of *The Adventure of the Speckled Band* by Sir
Arthur Conan Doyle.

Sherlock Holmes and Dr Watson meet Helen Stoner, whose
sister died unexpectedly two years earlier. Her last words
were "the speckled band!" Now Helen is hearing strange
noises at Stoke Moran, where she lives with her stepfather,
the impoverished Dr Roylott, who once lived in India.

Holmes examines Helen's mother's will, then he and Watson
spend the night in Helen's room. They discover that the
"speckled band" is a venomous snake. As it enters the room,
Holmes strikes it with a stick, driving it away. It then attacks
Roylott, who wanted his step-daughters' fortune.

Find out about another famous fictional mystery and write a
summary of the plot in less than 100 words.

....

....

....

....

....

....

....

....

....

....

....

....

Testing my skills

1. What are **two** synonyms for *influencer*?

   ● ....

   ● ....

2. *Trojan* is an adjective that relates to the city of Troy or its inhabitants. Can you think of **two** other uses of the word?

   ● ....

   ● ....

3. Which of the following words could reasonably be used to describe someone who is keen to learn about life in a positive way? Circle those which apply.

   A Gregarious

   B Obstinate

   C Vengeful

   D Forthright

4. *Philanthropy* is an interesting word. Which of these three definitions do you think is the most appropriate?

   A Being wealthy enough – perhaps a millionaire – to be able to give back to society

   B Having a heart of gold and always wanting to help people when you can

   C Giving very generous donations of money

5. Write a sentence on the theme of social media in which you use an adjective and a noun with the same stem. For example: I've met a lot of friendly people on social media, who are now my friends.

   ....

   ....

   ....

   ....

6. Which of these are figures of speech?

A When speaking about numbers ☐

B He had the fans eating out of his hands. ☐

C The hateful eight ☐

D All seasons shall be sweet to thee. ☐

E The cat just stood there motionless. ☐

7. You have been commissioned to write a drama series, but the producers have insisted you open the series with a sub-plot. Decide on your drama series, then say what the sub-plot will be and how it will add value to your series.

Drama series title: ....

Sub-plot: ....

....

....

....

Added value: ....

....

....

....

8. Where might you see a synopsis used rather than a more formal summary? Give **two** examples.

● ....

....

● ....

....

Dream destination

My favourite destination has to be Iceland. The people are so friendly, the landscape is stunning and Reykjavik is one of the most charming capital cities in the world. Where else can you step from one continent to another across a continental fault line? Or go whale watching in the morning, trek on a glacier in the afternoon and watch the Aurora Borealis (Northern Lights) after supper? And if that isn't enough, check out the original geyser that shoots hot steamy water 30 metres into the air or spend a relaxing few hours swimming in a thermal pool at the Blue Lagoon before indulging in a piece of blueberry skyr cheesecake, one of the local favourites.

1. What is your dream destination?

....

....

2. Using the passage on Iceland as a guide, write a short piece about your dream destination. Your aim is to persuade the reader to visit it.

....

....

....

....

....

....

....

....

....

3. Sum up in only three words the reasons why your dream destination is so special for you.

....

Design to persuade

Gran Roque has many delightful posadas.
These are hostels where guests can stay while
enjoying the many outside activities that Los
Roques offers.

Tourists can enjoy nature, snorkelling, scuba
diving and watching the sunset. Holidays make
minimal impact on the environment.

You are a hotel designer and you have been
commissioned to design an ecologically
friendly hotel with a theme based on the local
environment. Here is your brief:

- Your ideas should persuade guests to stay at your hotel.
- The hotel should make a minimal impact on the natural
  environment.
- You can choose the theme.
- The hotel must make guests feel that they are getting
  back to nature.

1. Decide on your theme and explain your choice.

   My theme is ....

   My reasons for choosing this theme are ....

   ....

   ....

   ....

2. Using a separate sheet of paper, design and draw a plan of
   one of the following:
   - the hotel lobby
   - a guest room
   - a restaurant

   Your plan should be labelled with the themed design
   features that make your hotel different.

   You might like to develop your ideas by writing notes before
   you start drawing your plan.

Using adjectives for effect

> Ecotourism is sensitive to the natural environment. It builds environmental awareness by visiting unspoilt places, preserving biological and cultural diversity. Indigenous people are empowered through sustainable and rewarding work.

1. Identify the adjectives in the paragraph above.

....

....

....

2. What do the adjectives suggest about the different impact of ecotourism?

....

....

....

💡 **Remember**

Adjectives:
- describe nouns by giving you more information
- come before a noun or after a verb in a phrase

3. Here are the adjectives used to describe another hotel:

flashy	expensive	wasteful	corporate
international	branded	plastic	fashionable
technological	electronic		

Using the adjectives in the box, write a paragraph describing this hotel in a way that persuades guests not to stay there.

....

....

....

....

....

....

....

Creating an image

In 'Our friend the moose', Bill Bryson describes the moose as charming but stupid to create a comic effect. However, in reality the animal is large, powerful and potentially dangerous.

Using the information below, on a separate sheet of paper, write a short article for a newspaper warning people to avoid contact with this dangerous animal. Call your article 'Beware of the moose!'

Moose facts

- The largest members of the deer family
- Strong runners
- Solitary animals
- Have a lifespan of about 17 years
- Can grow to 2.3 m tall
- Antler spread can be 2 m wide
- Have hoofed feet and large bodies

Moose effects

- Moose cause hundreds of motor accidents every year in North America and Europe – many of them are fatal for the drivers.

- As accidents are so frequent, the 'moose test' is a safety exam new cars must pass in Scandinavia.

- In Canada new highways must have anti-moose fences built by the roadside to protect motorists.

- Special road signs warn motorists to be careful of moose crossing roads.

- In Norway it is estimated there were 13,000 collisions between moose and trains between 2000 and 2008.

Using juxtaposition and oxymoron

Juxtaposition is placing two ideas or concepts next to each other to create a contrast or comparison.

→

The grand old town square dates back to the Middle Ages yet it is dotted with modern coffee chain outlets.

1. Explain the use of juxtaposition in these sentences.

a The towering volcano rises majestically above the drab little town below.

....

....

b City dwellers searching for the peace and serenity only an isolated cottage on a lonely hill can provide; those from a rural background desperate for the excitement and endless possibilities of the capital city.

....

....

c The freedom of an open rail ticket with no planned destination is appealing yet the thought of arriving in a foreign city with nowhere to stay and no idea where I am frightens me.

> **Remember**
>
> An oxymoron is a combination of apparently contradictory words that, when used together, create an image.

....

....

2. Why are these examples of oxymoron?

a hauntingly beautiful

....

b classically contemporary

....

c unbiased opinion

....

Modal verbs

The most common modal verbs are: *can* *could* *may* *might* *shall* *should* *will* *would*	Some of the functions of modal verbs are to: • describe what is possible, probable or certain • make a request or offer a suggestion.

1. Match the five functions of modal verbs in the box to the sentences below.

Functions of modal verbs

    A possibility   **B** probability   **C** certainty
    D Request   **E** Suggestion

a Might I trouble you for directions to the beach please? ....

b I can have your room ready for 3pm. ....

c The office is open until 5pm should you reconsider. ....

d I would be willing to save you two seats on the ship. ....

e I may be able to open an account for you. ....

f May I suggest you have dinner at the hotel? ....

g There will be no problem with booking today. ....

h Could you tell me where the station is? ....

2. Using the theme of travel as a subject, create a sentence using a modal verb for each of these functions.

a Possibility: ....

b Probability: ....

c Certainty: ....

d Request: ....

e Suggestion: ....

3. In the following pairs of modal verbs, which suggests a stronger expression?

a *Can* or *will* ....   **b** *Might* or *could* ....

Writing to persuade — a travel blog

Knowing the place you are going to write about is very important. Start with somewhere you have been often and can describe in detail from memory. What seems everyday and commonplace to you will be exciting and new to a tourist from far away.

Key features of travel blogs

- Non-fiction text
- Describe a personal experience
- Use detail to engage the reader
- Presentation and arrangement should be colourful and exciting
- Use images as well as written text

1. In the box write all the good features of your home town (or country). Try to include as many as you can. Around the edge of the box write all the places you think a visitor should visit.

2. Choose one or two ideas from your box and use them as the basis for a short persuasive paragraph promoting your chosen place.

....

....

....

....

....

Testing my skills

1. Why is ecotourism different from a normal package holiday?

....

....

2. Which kind of descriptive words are used to persuade tourists that their holiday will be different and memorable?

....

....

3. 'Where else can you step from one continent to another across a continental fault line? Or go whale watching in the morning, trek on a glacier in the afternoon and watch the Aurora Borealis (Northern Lights) after supper?'

Circle the features that make this an effective piece of travel writing.

A Rhetorical questions **D** Good content

B Long sentences **E** Use of details

C Iceland is cool

4. Complete this paragraph by inserting the appropriate adjectives.

If you visit the Serengeti, leopards are the hardest to spot of all predators as these **(a)** .... animals find trees and secluded places are **(b)** .... locations to hide and sleep. They are naturally **(c)** .... Other wild animals you can find in this **(d)** .... Northern Tanzanian nature reserve include **(e)** .... buffalo and **(f)** .... gazelles. In contrast, herds of wildebeest can be found everywhere on the **(g)** .... plains searching for something **(h)** .... but these awkward and **(i)** .... creatures are neither quick, nor impressive nor elegant. They look permanently **(j)** .... without the defence of their herd, making them easy prey for the predators.

5. Why do writers use juxtaposition and oxymoron in their descriptions? Circle all that apply.

  A To showcase terminology

  B To create memorable and vivid images

  C To create structural contrasts

  D Use more adjectives

6. Below is an extract from a report making recommendations about environmentally friendly holidays. In each gap, insert the best modal verb from the list in the box.

> can   could   should   might   may

How could you make your tourism low impact and sustainable? You **(a)** .... consider carbon offset to balance out the environmental cost of your travel. You **(b)** .... choose a destination unspoilt by mass tourism where development is sensitive to the needs of the local population and habitat. Your destination **(c)** .... include activities which support local sustainability projects, such as conservation of resources. You **(d)** .... wish to consider what you leave behind, as well as what you take from your destination. Wherever you choose to go, you **(e)** .... make a decision to have a positive environmental impact.

7. What is the most important thing to remember when a short-answer question asks you to refer to an extract to find the answer? Rank the importance of these three ways (1 is the most important, 3 is the least important).

Use quotation marks ☐

Copy something out ☐

Use your own words ☐

8. What do we call the skill of working out facts that are not explicitly stated but follow on from something you have read and understood? Tick (✔) the correct answer.

Summary ☐   Inference ☐

Synthesis ☐   Recall ☐

Recognising text types

What kind of text does each of the following extracts come from? For each one, identify the features that helped you to recognise it.

1.

> The ostrich is the biggest bird alive today. It has a height of 2.5 metres – as tall as a football goalpost. It has a very long neck and the largest eyes of all land animals with backbones. An ostrich can run extremely fast. Unlike most birds, however, it cannot fly.

Text type ....

Features ....

2.

> When she awakened she lay and stared at the wall. The house was perfectly still. She had never known it to be so silent before. She heard neither voices nor footsteps, and wondered if everybody had got well of the cholera and all the trouble was over.
>
> From *The Secret Garden* by Frances Hodgson Burnett

Text type ....

Features ....

3.

> Break the chocolate into a medium-sized heatproof bowl. To melt the chocolate, fit the bowl over a saucepan of very hot water. You can do this off the heat for safety, but it will take a little time. Stir the chocolate. Cut the butter in little pieces and add it to the chocolate, stirring until it is melted.
>
> From *Eats for Treats* by Jane Asher

Text type ....

Features ....

4.

> So here I stand . . . one girl among many. I speak – not for myself, but for all girls and boys. I raise up my voice – not so that I can shout, but so that those without a voice can be heard. Those who have fought for their rights. Their right to live in peace. Their right to be treated with dignity. Their right to equality of opportunity. Their right to be educated.
>
> From Malala Yousafzai's speech at the Youth Takeover of the United Nations, July 2013

Text type ....

Features ....

New words

The English language is constantly changing, with new words being introduced, and some words disappearing from use. The word *selfie* was first included in the Oxford English Dictionary in 2013. In 2014, *mahoosive*, *jel* and *al desko*, among others, were included in dictionaries and in 2015, *uber*, *FOMO*, *crowdfund* and *hyperlocal*.

1. Make a list of as many 'new' words as you can. For each one, explain what it means and suggest where it might have come from.

    ....

    ....

    ....

    ....

2. Now think about and list some words that are disappearing or have disappeared from everyday use. (Tip – parents, teachers or other older people might give you some help here!)

    ....

    ....

    ....

    ....

3. Finally, think about words where the meaning has changed or that have different meanings, for example, *mouse*. Make a list and explain the different meanings of each word.

    ....

    ....

    ....

    ....

Figurative language

1. Complete the table to show which figurative technique is used in each example and the text type it might have come from. (Warning: there may be more than one possibility!)

   S = simile   M = metaphor
   P = personification   A = alliteration

Example	S	M	P	A	The text type it might have come from
Luscious lemon lollies					
The sea is a hungry dog, giant and grey					
The spider's web was like a delicate piece of lace					
Dozy Dave does it again!					
A silence crept into the classroom					
Key battleground for this election					

2. Now write an advertisement for a new chocolate bar and aim to include a simile, a metaphor, an example of alliteration and an example of personification.

   ....

   ....

   ....

   ....

   ....

   ....

Role-play – a podcast

Imagine someone has just come back from exploring a remote part of the planet (or another planet, if you like).

1. Think about where the explorer has been, what they were investigating and any key experiences he or she had while they were there. Write your ideas in the space below.

....

....

....

....

....

2. Think of at least three questions a podcaster might ask the explorer or another relevant person, who could be the explorer's relative, an expert on that part of the world or the person who rescued the explorer when they got into difficulties.

....

....

....

3. a Show your idea to a family member or friend. Decide which one of you is going to be the interviewer, and who is going to be the explorer or other relevant person.

   b Using the ideas and questions you have written above as a starting point, try to keep the interview going after these questions have been answered, making up new questions and ideas as you think of them.

   c Write down anything new and interesting you learn about the explorer's experiences as a result of the role-play.

....

....

....

....

Sentence combining

1. Combine the sentences below into one sentence in three different ways. You can change and add words if you like.

- Jon was late for school.
- He was very apologetic.
- The teacher gave him a detention.

....

....

....

2. Look at the sentences below and decide what order they should go in. Then write them out as a paragraph.

- The boy was small.
- He laughed with pleasure.
- The window was icy.
- He had tousled hair.
- He had never seen snowflakes before.
- He peered out of the window.

....

....

....

....

3. Now combine the sentences in different ways: into three sentences, two sentences and one sentence. You can change or add words, but you must include all the information.

Three sentences: ....

....

Two sentences: ....

....

One sentence: ....

....

Planning and proofreading

1. Choose one of the following topics and write a plan for a piece of writing.

- My favourite place of all time
- Why you should visit the area where I live
- A letter to someone explaining the advantages and disadvantages of living where you do

2. Proofread this sample answer. Mark all the errors you spot. Then write some feedback to help the writer make fewer errors in his next piece of writing.

My trip to Venice!

We arrived to the airport in the evening as it is getting dark. Then we got a water taxi across the lagoon to Venice itself. It is amazing! Ill never for the trip up the grand canal, all the lights twinkling. It was magical.

When we got to our hotel, it was late although everything was amazing. The bedroom is huge, it had a bed, a chair a desk and a TV. The bath had a Jacuzzi. Im loving it already. So, after a drink we went to bed

The next day we went out on a gondola and saw lot of old buildings, they were stuning. I liked the Doges' Palace best of all but my Mum like St Marks' Square. It was very crowd there, there were so many people my sisters bag was stolen. she was annoyed although she didn't like it very much and they had no money in them.

Feedback: ....

....

....

Comparing texts

Read the two texts below and complete the Venn diagram to
show the similarities and differences between them.

Text A

Penguins are the most common bird in Antarctica and are highly evolved
to be able to live in the coldest of places. All Antarctic penguins have a
striking black and white coat: some are just black and white, some have
yellow patches, and others have coloured eyebrows. All penguins have
similar body form and structure, but they vary greatly in size, from the
little penguin weighing 1.1 kg and about 40 cm tall, to the emperor penguin,
which weighs up to 40 kg and is about 115 cm tall. Although they have
wings and feathers, penguins cannot fly. Instead, they have evolved into
the most efficient swimmers and divers of all birds.

Text B

You can smell the penguins almost before you see them. The pong is
unbelievable! It's like being buried in a vat of old fish remains. Overpowering.
As we land, the sun is coming up, rosy pink against the blue-white of the
mountains and glaciers. As well as penguins, there are elephant seals – and
the glimpse of a whale in the distance. It is wildlife heaven! The penguins
chatter away to each other, oblivious to us – perhaps speculating on what
they'll catch today. I watch as one dives neatly into the icy sea and swims
powerfully out of sight. Perfect penguins!

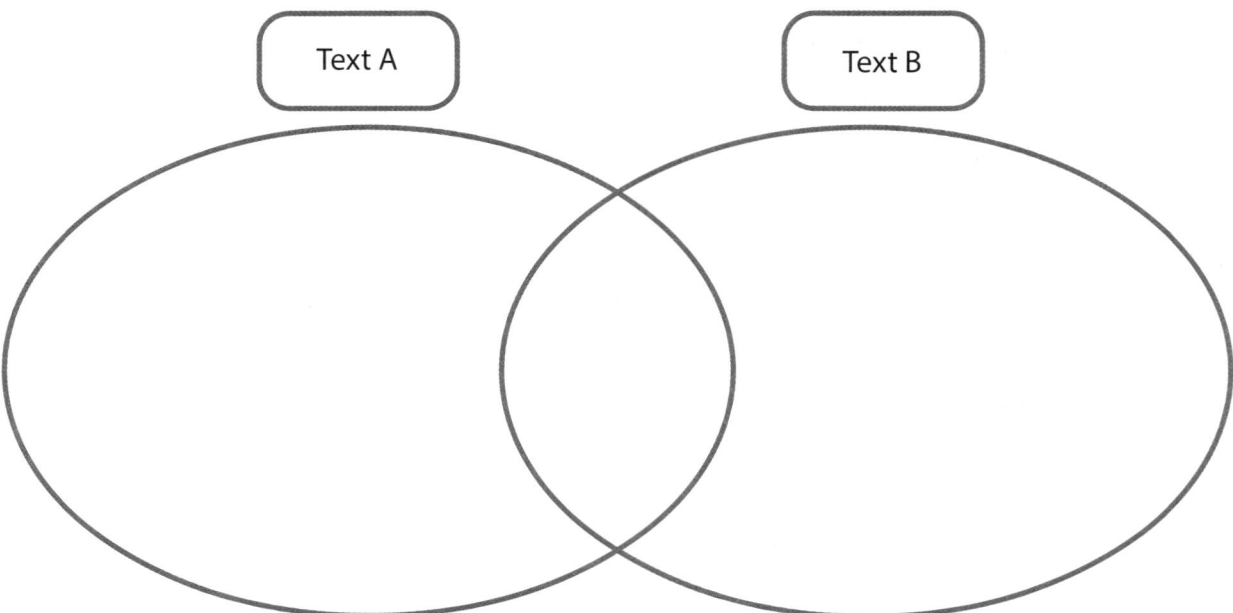

Text A

Text B

Testing my skills

1. Why is exploration different from tourism?

   ....

   ....

2. Which form of non-narrative writing is usually written in the third person?

   ....

3. Which of these words is a more interesting word to use than *sunny*? Tick (✓) one answer.

   somnolent ☐

   torrential ☐

   ominous ☐

   brilliant ☐

4. Why are rhetorical questions so effective in persuasive writing?

   ....

   ....

   ....

   ....

5. Why do journalists in news articles use figurative language? Circle all that apply.

   A Create pictures in the reader's mind

   B Make their writing flow

   C To showcase writer's effects

   D Compare something unfamiliar to something familiar

6. Change the order of this sentence to emphasise the importance of challenge and adventure.

> *Young people need challenges and adventures in order to help them develop their self-confidence.*

....

....

....

....

7. What are the most important things to think about in non-narrative writing? Tick (✓) one answer.

Entertainment and engagement ☐

Purpose and audience ☐

Facts and details ☐

8. What do we call the skill of reflecting on what you have learned from different sources and developing ideas in your own way? Tick (✓) one answer.

Analysis ☐

Exposition ☐

Synthesis ☐

Evaluation ☐

Identifying key ideas

Look at the United Nations flag and the key ideas within it.

Key ideas

- White emblem on blue background
- Map of the world
- Map set within five concentric circles
- Map surrounded by a wreath of olive branches signifying world peace

1. Here are two more flags used by organisations within the United Nations. Both are white on a blue background.

Flag A

Flag B

Look at the following key ideas about the flags. Write **A** or **B** (or both) against each statement to show which flag it matches.

a The Greek temple represents science, learning and culture. ☐

b The twin anchors represent the sea. ☐

c The wreath of olive leaves symbolises peace. ☐

d Blue and white are the official UN colours. ☐

e UNESCO is an acronym for United Nations Educational, Scientific and Cultural Organization. ☐

f Represents IMO (International Maritime Organization) ☐

g Map of the world ☐

2. On a separate sheet of paper, list the key ideas about each organisation that can be inferred from the flag that represents it.

Expanding your vocabulary – low-frequency words

One way to expand your vocabulary is to use more low-frequency words. Low-frequency words are those that are used less often.

The following words were all used in the article about the Mozart effect on pages 106–107 of the Student Book. Some of them are considered low-frequency words.

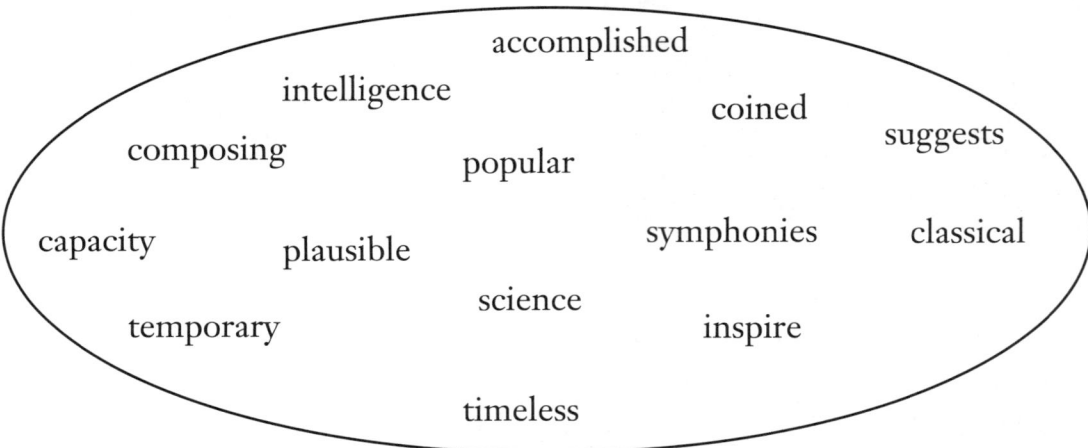

accomplished

intelligence

coined

suggests

composing

popular

capacity

plausible

symphonies

classical

science

temporary

inspire

timeless

You may need to use a dictionary to complete these exercises.

1. Underline the words you think are low-frequency.

2. Choose one word you think is low-frequency and one you think is high-frequency. Explain your reasons for choosing each.

Low-frequency word: ....

Reason: ....

....

High-frequency word: ....

Reason: ....

....

3. Choose three other words you have identified as being low-frequency. Give an alternative high-frequency word for each one.

Low-frequency word	High-frequency alternative

Using topic sentences

A topic sentence:
- is the most important sentence in a paragraph
- introduces the main idea in the paragraph.

A topic sentence is useful because:
- it focuses the writing within the paragraph
- it indicates to the reader what the paragraph will be about.

This is a brief summary of the main points in an article about gaining more freedom by expanding your brain's cognitive (thinking) capacity.

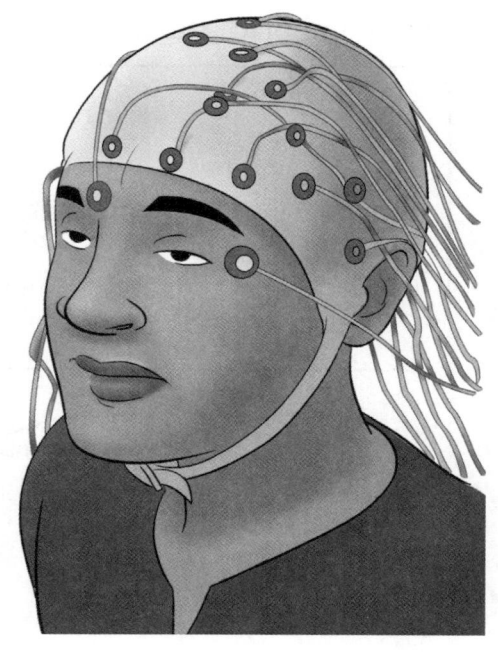

'Humans only use ten per cent of their mental capacity.' Does any scientific evidence support this idea? The theory began in the late 19th century and was supported by leading figures in science for more than half a century. Advertising, authors of fiction and movie directors have all used the theory to support their projects. Studies have considered the use of music to increase mental capacity. Certain foods are thought to increase brain activity. Scientific study today suggests the theory is an urban myth. There is no scientific basis to suggest we only use ten per cent of the brain's capacity. In fact, we use all the brain's capacity. There is no easy way to increase it.

The complete article contains five paragraphs. Use the summary to write an appropriate topic sentence for each paragraph.

Introduction ....

....

Second paragraph ....

....

Third paragraph ....

....

Fourth paragraph ....

....

Conclusion ....

....

Concrete and abstract nouns

Nouns can be concrete or abstract.

> **Concrete nouns:** the names of things that can be identified by one of the five senses so they can be seen, touched, heard, tasted or smelt.

> **Abstract nouns:** the names of feelings, ideals, concepts and qualities that cannot be identified by sight, touch, hearing, taste or smell.

Decide whether the following words are concrete or abstract nouns and place them in the correct circle.

doctor	syringe	hospital	jealousy	medicine
kindness	intelligence	patience	patient	
country	border	calm	epidemic	surprise
loyalty	pride	disaster	flood	
bandage	weakness	uniform	stethoscope	tiredness
		nurse		

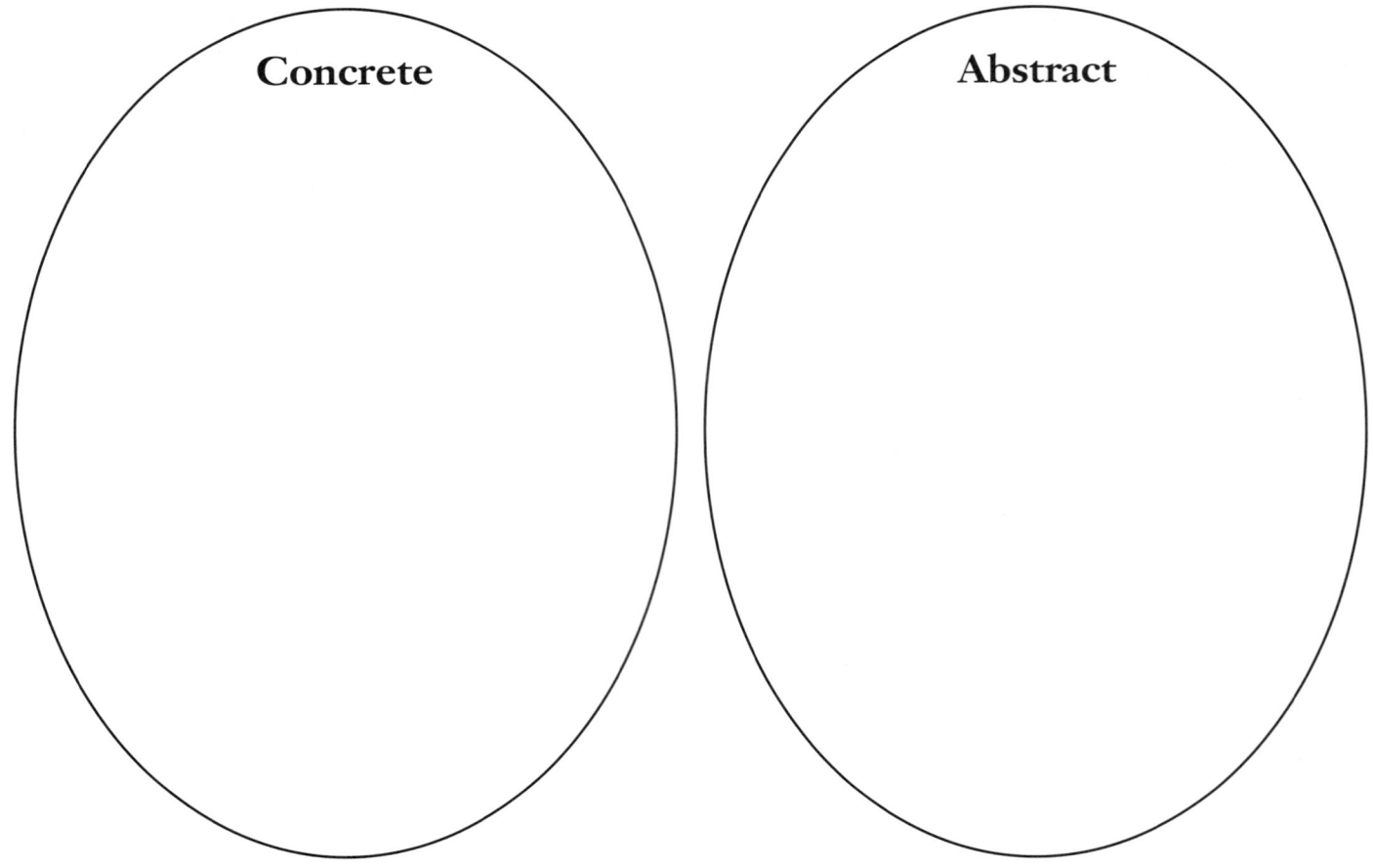

Concrete   **Abstract**

Transitions

Transitions are words and phrases used to connect ideas in writing.

1. There are six transitions in the following extract. Find all six.

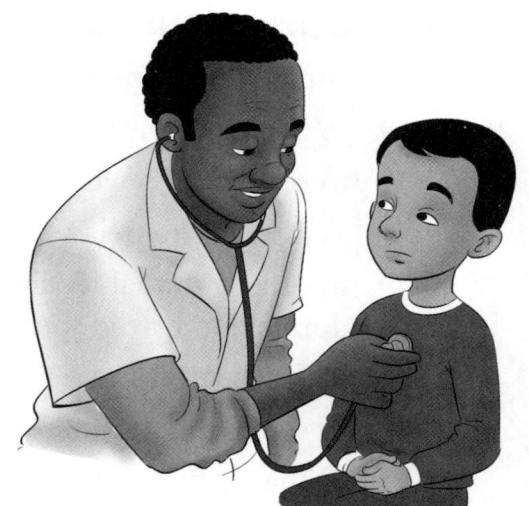

> First of all Médecins Sans Frontières applies scientific and medical knowledge for the purpose of charity. As a result the doctors, nurses and support workers volunteer their time without pay. In the same way as other charities, MSF sends its volunteers where they are most needed. They often work in dangerous places, in particular war zones, so their lives are often in danger and yet these brave people continue to offer their services to help others. Furthermore, they do not consider themselves to be heroes but just normal people with skills that can be used to help make bad situations better.

2. Match each transition on the right to the correct description of its use on the left. One is already completed for you.

Transitions are used to:	Transition used in extract:
Order or sequence events	furthermore
Add information	first of all
Show cause and effect	and yet
Show emphasis/illustrate	as a result
Contrast	in the same way
Compare	in particular

3. Write a short paragraph about an application of science you are familiar with, using four of the transitions from the list above.

....

....

....

....

Discourse markers

The main functions of discourse markers are:

- to begin a topic in a conversation
- to refocus a conversation
- as fillers or to delay speaking
- to offer minimal feedback during a conversation dominated by the speaker
- to focus attention on what is to come in the sentence
- to signal the attitude or point of view being expressed.

Erm, did I mean to say that?

1. Read the six functions again, then cover the list. Now try to remember them by repeating them out loud.

   Could you remember them all without hesitating or did you use discourse markers to help you think?

Discourse markers occur more often in speech than in writing because some kinds are unintentional or unplanned.

2. Look at the following scenarios and decide whether each discourse marker is planned for a purpose or unplanned and spontaneous. Write **P** for planned or **U** for unplanned by each one.

   a 'Okay, I am now going to address a different topic.'

   b 'I am struggling to remember the details… I think it was a Monday evening.'

   c 'Exactly', 'Absolutely', 'Yes' – all in response to the main speaker.

   d 'Now, this is the important part…'

   e 'Understandably, I am not a great fan of that point of view.'

   f 'On the other hand, I am aware that there is a different point of view that is valid.'

3. Have a five-minute conversation with a family member or friend. Make a note below of the discourse markers used.

....

....

....

....

Writing an effective argument

As with any piece of sustained writing, the most important stage is planning.

Imagine you have been asked to write a plan for an argumentative essay. It has to be on a controversial subject so you may want to ask your parents or friends to suggest topics.

Take one side of the argument. Use the planning boxes to map out a plan for your essay.

Paragraph 1 – Introduction (An overview of the argument, introducing the points to support your opinion)

Paragraph 2 – Your first supportive point

Paragraph 3 – Your second supportive point

Paragraph 4 – The counter-argument (Reasons that are against what you are arguing)

Paragraph 5 – Your conclusion (Sum up your points)

Testing my skills

1. If a school claimed that 'Our school has students powered by new technologies and the opportunities they bring', what language device is the writer using?

   ....

2. Look at these two examples. Which is more effective in a scientific argument? Circle your answer and explain why you made your choice.

   A Listening to Mozart might make you cleverer and can even give you an emotional high.

   B Particular patterns in Mozart's music may activate cortical cerebral circuits; experiment suggests accelerated mental processing for humans could be achieved.

   ....

   ....

   ....

3. Which part of speech is the word *spatial*? Circle the one correct answer.

   A Noun

   B Adverb

   C Adjective

   D Preposition

4. Which of the following is a topic sentence? Tick (✓) the correct answer.

   A Although the effect was only temporary, it was enough to arouse widespread attention. ☐

   B In the years that followed, right up to today, the Mozart effect has remained a popular theory. ☐

   C Furthermore, in a separate study by the University of Electronic Science and Technology of China, it was revealed to be false. ☐

   D The magic of Mozart was truly casting its spell. ☐

5. Fill in the gaps in the text below with an adverb or adjective formed from each of the following words: *historic, chunk, reuse, rigorous*.

Richard Branson's first space flight is **(a)** .... important because it shows space tourism is for anyone.

However, he needed to prepare **(b)** .... and heftily invested his own money. If you are prepared to pay a **(c)** .... price, you too could travel on a

(d) .... rocket into outer space.

6. Which of these transitions are used to show cause and effect? Circle two answers.

   A Furthermore

   B To conclude

   C Consequently

   D Subsequently

   E Hence

7. Which of these discourse markers is the most appropriate to refocus a conversation? Tick (✓) the correct answer.

   A On the other hand   ☐

   B As far as I am concerned   ☐

   C Absolutely   ☐

   D Well, you know   ☐

8. Open questions are especially helpful to speakers who have given presentations. Give two functions of open questions:

   ● ....

   ● ....

Talking about poetry

Poetry is a creative art form which is different from a short story or a novel. During this course you will have studied a number of poems and this is a chance to talk about what you understand about poems.

Find someone to talk to about your experience of poems and to discuss your opinions with you.

Here are some things to discuss:

- How is a poem different from a short story or a novel?
- How do poems create pictures in words?
- Which sorts of poems do you like or dislike reading?
- Can you write poems? What do you think you have to be able to do to write a poem?
- Are poems best read silently or aloud?

When you have finished, write some of your thoughts about poems here:

....

....

....

....

....

....

....

....

On the right is the Mouse's long and sad tale from *Alice's Adventures in Wonderland* by Lewis Carroll. A visual poem such as this is called a calligram. You can write poems in shapes as well as verses. Use any shape you like.

Fury said to a
mouse that
he met in
the house,
"Let us
both go to
law: *I*
will prosecute
you. Come,
I'll take no
denial: we
must have a
trial: for
really this
morning
I've noth-
ing to do."
Said the
mouse to
the cur,
"Such a
trial, dear
sir, with
no jury
or judge,
would be
wasting
our
breath."
"I'll be
judge, I'll
be jury,"
said
cun-
ning
old
Fury:
"I'll
try
the
whole
cause,
and
con-
demn
you to
death."

Scary!

Many people are afraid of all sorts of creatures. In the two snake poems you read, neither of the writers seemed bothered by snakes at all. Some people can't stay in the same room as a cat – other people love them. Not many people love spiders, though – especially when they are poisonous ones that you discover in a box of bananas. Don't be ashamed of being afraid because you will always find other people exactly like you: you're never alone!

Write about being frightened of an animal or an insect. In paragraph 1, introduce your writing by making some general comments about people and their fears and what you think causes them. In paragraph 2, write about your own personal fear of some creature or other.

Making notes and giving a short talk

1. Read this text about wolves and make a list of five facts it tells you about this predator.

> The grey wolf, also known as the timber wolf, lives in remote, wild areas of the world. It is a gregarious and social animal which travels in complete families including its adult offspring. It has few enemies other than humans and tigers. Although the grey wolf is feared by humans, attacks are extremely rare, because it lives far away from people and has learned to avoid them. Although it is called a grey wolf, its colour can vary from white through all shades to black, and it has a special winter coat which it sheds each spring. Wolves attack their prey in groups and can kill large animals such as elk and deer; they are infamous for taking sheep. They will also scavenge and eat tiny animals such as mice.

For each fact you find write no more than six words.

Fact 1 ....

Fact 2 ....

Fact 3 ....

Fact 4 ....

Fact 5 ....

2. Now prepare a short talk you might give about grey wolves. Make your brief notes on this page. Never read your notes when giving the talk, but keep them handy in case you need a prompt.

....

....

....

....

....

....

....

Crocodiles – a reality check

How doth the little crocodile
Improve his shining tail,
And pour the waters of the Nile
On every golden scale!

How cheerfully he seems to grin,
How neatly spreads his claws,
And welcome little fishes in
With gently smiling jaws!

Lewis Carroll

1. In what ways does this little poem present an unrealistic picture of a crocodile?

....

....

....

2. How is it funny?

....

....

....

3. Find out some interesting facts about crocodiles and then write your answer to Lewis Carroll in the same verse and rhyme form. Write about what crocodiles are *really* like.

....

....

....

....

....

....

It's those full stops again!

This is just a reminder that you can't put commas between sentences. Lots of people get it wrong, so it's a good idea to get some more practice. Can you see what's wrong with this sentence?

It must be very frightening to go for a nice swim and suddenly to see a pointed fin coming up behind you, it is most probably a hungry shark.

This is wrong because *it* doesn't join two sentences. It should be:

It must be very frightening to go for a nice swim and suddenly to see a pointed fin coming up behind you. It is most probably a hungry shark. (Remember the capital letter for *It*.)

1. Add the correct punctuation in the following sentences.

   a The most scary thing about sharks is their teeth they have three tiers of them and they are exceedingly sharp

   b You may think that sharks are a single species in fact there are 500 different sorts

   c The smallest shark is the dwarf lanternshark it is only seventeen centimetres long

   d The whale shark is the biggest fish in the world this shark can be twelve metres long

   e A man was attacked by a shark he escaped by beating it off with his surfboard

2. Now write a few sentences to describe a quiet lake which is suddenly disturbed by a huge creature. Check that you have used full stops correctly.

....

....

....

....

....

....

....

The Kraken

Below the thunders of the upper deep;
Far, far beneath in the abysmal sea,
His ancient, dreamless, uninvaded sleep
The Kraken sleepeth: faintest sunlights flee
About his shadowy sides: above him swell
Huge sponges of millennial growth and height;
And far away into the sickly light,
From many a wondrous grot and secret cell

Unnumber'd and enormous polypi
Winnow with giant arms the slumbering green.
There hath he lain for ages and will lie
Battening upon huge seaworms in his sleep,
Until the latter fire shall heat the deep;
Then once by man and angels to be seen,
In roaring he shall rise and on the surface die.

Alfred Lord Tennyson

The Kraken was a legendary monster of huge proportions believed to live off the coasts of Norway and Greenland

Tennyson imagines a creature that does not exist in a place under the sea where he has never been.

1. What does Tennyson think it is like at the bottom of the sea? Which words does he use to create his picture?

....

....

....

....

....

2. The creatures that live at the bottom of the sea seem to be very big. How does Tennyson give you this impression?

....

....

....

....

Expressing more preferences — town or country?

Where would you like to live? In the middle of a busy town with hustle and bustle but with all your favourite shops and places to go, or in the middle of the countryside, surrounded by trees, animals and insects?

Decide which you prefer. Write a paragraph about the advantages of living where you want. Then write a paragraph about the disadvantages of living in the other place.

....

....

....

....

....

....

....

....

....

....

....

....

....

....

....

....

....

....

Testing my skills

1. Here are some statements about poetry but only one of them is correct. Tick (✓) one answer.

   Poetry always has to rhyme. ☐

   Poetry has to be written in verses of the same length. ☐

   Poetry can be written in many different forms, shapes and structures. ☐

2. What is the term used to describe verses consisting of three lines? Circle the correct answer.

   Couplets   Triplets   Stanzas   Quatrains

3. What language feature is being used in this line of poetry?

   > *I'd never bake a cake containing a filling of snake.*

   ....

4. In a sentence, what is the difference between a main clause and a subordinate clause?

   ....

   ....

   ....

5. Complete the following complex sentences using a suitable conjunction for each one.

   My favourite poem by Blake is 'The Tyger' .... of the superb imagery.

   I love to read poetry at any time of the day .... on my own.

6. What is wrong with this sentence?

   > *Lambs are so innocent, they make you want to protect them.*

   ....

   ....

   ....

7. For opinions to be taken seriously they have to be responsible. Which one of these opinions is the most responsible? Tick (✓) one answer.

   A No, I'm not interested because it's rubbish! ☐

   B On reflection, the Melville poem seems more realistic than the Blake poem so for me it is much more enjoyable. ☐

   C Well maybe I'd choose it but I still think it's really boring. ☐

   D I like the snake poem better as it rhymes. ☐

8. Find four features of persuasive writing used in this extract. Justify your answers with evidence from the text.

> *I love zoos. When I was a young girl my father would take me to see the penguins being fed. Those cute little sideways wobbling movements they made when they hurried over to the fish bucket always made me laugh aloud. How could you not fall in love with those creatures? Every now and then one would stop, look around and seem to think 'man, this is the life' before scooting off into the pool with its prized dinner. Penguins are great and deserve to be protected. We need to make sure they are.*

- ....
....
....

- ....
....
....

- ....
....
....

- ....
....
....

Two speaking activities

One minute please

This game can be played by a small number of people of any age. You need a stopwatch.

The chairperson gives you a topic and you must speak for one minute without pausing, without repeating yourself, and without straying off the subject.

Any player can challenge you. If the chairperson doesn't allow the challenge, you score one point. If the challenger is successful, he/she scores a point and continues the topic. The person speaking at the end of one minute scores two points.

Here is a simple score card:

Player number

1 ....

2 ....

3 ....

4 ....

Character monologue

A monologue means one person speaking without being interrupted.

This is a drama activity. You need to act the part of a person with a particular characteristic and speak for as long as you can to your parent or a friend.

Choose one of the words in the box to describe the person whose character you are portraying.

greedy	kind
nervous	proud
bad-tempered	careless
conceited	peculiar
enthusiastic	forgetful

If several people are taking part, write the words on separate slips of paper and pick one up from the pile so that you speak spontaneously.

List the words you have used:

....

....

Why context is important

1. Explain the meaning of each of the words below. You will need to look at the context to be sure of the meaning.

   a   A *match* can mean a game of two sides. It can also have other meanings.

   > Everyone said that Tony and Iris were a perfect match, and he was standing at mid-on during the teachers' cricket match when the ball came towards him and he had to dive. He caught the ball, but the matches in his pocket caught fire and the poor man had to be put out!

   Match can also mean:

   ....

   ....

   b   Two men were walking through a wood when one said 'Duck!' and the other said 'Where?'

   Duck can mean:

   ....

   and: ....

2. Now suppose you don't know the meaning of the word *point-blank*. Study the context to find a hint.

   > He went to the boss and pleaded for more money, but he was met with a point-blank refusal and went away empty handed and very angry.

   Point-blank means:

   ....

3. > A politician said "I am totally against giving money unconditionally to international aid. I am therefore instructing government departments only to contribute to actual projects and not to political organisations." The next day a newspaper reported the speech on the front page with the headline, 'Minister is totally against giving money to international aid'.

   The minister was angry and said his words had been taken out of context. Explain.

   ....

   ....

Describing a character

Choose one of these pictures and describe the character you see. Use the present tense and include these things in your writing:

- what they look like
- what their characteristics are
- what they might say and do if you met them.

The name of my character is ....

....

....

....

....

....

....

....

....

....

....

Writer's attitude – seeing through different eyes

Here are two extracts from diary entries. They are written by two people who visited the same town centre at the same time of day.

When I got to the precinct it was raining a bit, but that did not matter, I stopped to look at the new fountain – a good piece of public architecture and the kids love playing round it. There was a group of teenagers chatting away in front of the supermarket entrance. I couldn't help joining in as it was all about my favourite football team. They gave me a smile but must have thought it a bit odd, a person of my age interrupting!

Raining as usual – I got soaked. Mind you, most of the water came from that ugly fountain and the stupid kids splashing round it. I blame the parents. I don't like supermarkets at the best of times, and certainly not when there are wretched teenage nuisances blocking the entrance. Pity someone doesn't give them a job to do. We oldies don't want them scowling at us wherever we go.

1. What sort of people wrote these two diary entries? How are their attitudes towards their visits and the people they came across different?

   ....

   ....

   ....

   ....

2. What facts do you learn from reading the two extracts? What is the truth of what the town centre was like and what was happening? Is either account truthful?

   ....

   ....

   ....

   ....

   ....

   ....

   ....

Practising your sentences

1. Read the following extract from a letter and identify which of the sentences is simple, which is coordinated and which is compound.

Dear Hatya

(a) I had a marvellous time in the Gobi Desert. (b) The weather was warm and the people welcomed me with open arms. (c) When it was night-time we all slept in a yurt which had plenty of room for everybody.

a ....

b ....

c ....

Did you notice how the writer used different types and lengths of sentences as she wrote?

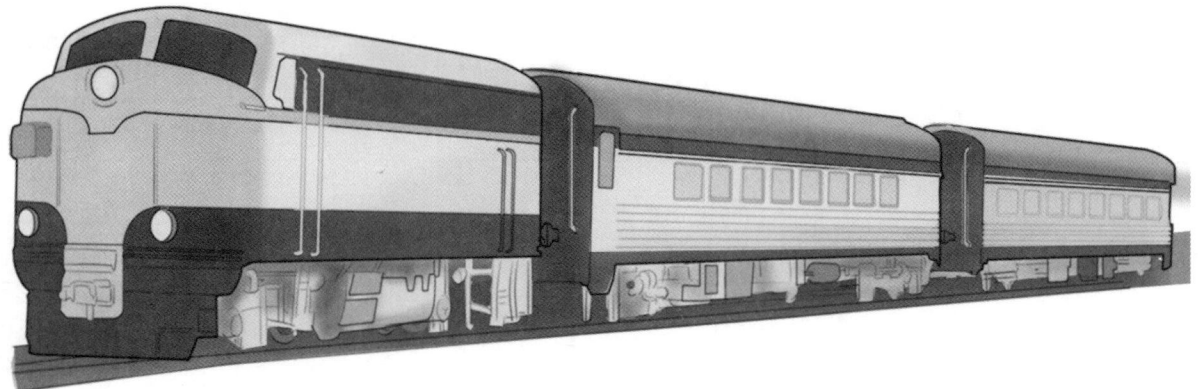

2. Make these simple sentences into one compound sentence. Remember the order of the sentences can be changed.

a The rains do not come. Everyone yearns for water. They need to grow crops to survive.

....

....

....

b May I introduce you to my uncle? He has been a teacher at the secondary school. It opened over twenty years ago.

....

....

....

Why do we need to have group discussions?

At times, we all need to share ideas with other people and come to some agreed decisions. One of the topics that families with teenagers often disagree on is where to go on the annual vacation. What adults want from a holiday is not necessarily the same thing as what teenagers want.

Find two people at home with whom you can discuss where it would be good to spend a holiday and why.

Keep some notes and, at the end of the discussion, write the following:

1. What different people thought

....

....

....

....

....

2. What we decided

....

....

....

....

....

3. How effectively did I make my views known to the others?

....

....

....

....

....

Starting a story by describing an interesting character

Write the opening of a story about two children who are exploring a forest path when suddenly they come face to face with the strangest old woman they have ever met.

Start your story with these words: There was something about the woman that made the children stop in their tracks.

Here is a bank of words that you can use to describe the old woman. You need not use all the words.

wizened	straggly hair	mysterious
piercing eyes	powerful voice	magical
sardonic smile	demanded	spine-chilling
aggressive	hungry-looking	sinister
crinkled skirt	haunted	bony nose

....

....

....

....

....

....

....

....

....

....

....

....

....

....

Testing my skills

1. Why is understanding context important when interpreting what an unfamiliar word in an extract means? Tick (✓) one answer.

It shows the spelling is correct. ☐

It gives clues to the meaning of the word. ☐

It makes the word stand out better. ☐

2. When is it advisable to use non-standard English for a character in a story?

....

....

3. Turn these two simple sentences into one coordinated sentence.

> *The Gobi Desert is a hostile environment. It is very hard to exist there.*

....

....

....

4. Complete the following sentences.

   a I'm the most important part of a compound sentence and they call me a .... clause.

   b Okay, I'm different. I'm like a sentence, but I don't make sense by myself. I'm less important, so they call me a .... clause.

5. Complete each of these sentences using a suitable conjunction from the list. Only one conjunction fits each sentence.

> which   until   who   since

   a Nomads are travellers .... do not have a permanent home in any one place.

b Horses are the most beloved possessions of nomads .... makes them very valuable.

c Nomadic herdsmen will travel for miles across the desert .... they find a suitable water supply.

d Every nomad learns to ride a horse expertly .... their existence depends on such skill.

6. What is the primary task of the chairperson in a discussion? Circle one answer only.

To keep it in order

To ask questions

To keep notes

To manage time

7. When creating a character for a story, which of these is important to include? Circle all that apply.

Appearance

Personality

Mannerisms

Speech

8. Creating a convincing character can make a story more successful. What qualities make this description convincing?

> *Shuffling with the movement of one whose life had been dictated by decades of hard work and toil, Maria's aunt slowly manoeuvred towards the door. Her stooping shoulders made her seem shorter, more fragile. A wizened old crow, Maria thought. The image was further intensified by the eyes. Her aunt gazed unerringly at her niece as if deciding whether this worm was worthy of her attention.*

....

....

....

....

....

....

Soapbox!

This speaking and listening activity is designed to build up your confidence about speaking aloud in front of other people – and have some fun!

Decide on a controversial statement to talk about. Here are some examples. Don't just copy these, though you can adapt one to use yourself.

> School uniform should be banned.

> Nobody should be allowed to keep pets.

> Weekends should be three days long.

> Teenagers should be able to choose whether to go to school.

> Men should do all the cooking in the home.

> Teachers will soon be unnecessary because of the Internet.

Make notes for a one-minute speech based on your controversial statement. You have three minutes to do this – time yourself!

Find a friend or family member to make your speech to. Ask them to give you feedback based on how long you can keep going and how convincingly you argue your case.

Use the space below to make notes. Try to use some of the features of speeches you have learned about.

....

....

....

....

....

....

Humour in texts

1. In this extract, Pip, the hero, recalls a terrifying encounter with a dangerous criminal in a graveyard which he experienced as a boy.

> "You young dog," said the man, licking his lips, "what fat cheeks you ha' got." I believe they were fat, though I was at that time undersized for my years, and not strong.
>
> "Darn me if I couldn't eat 'em," said the man, with a threatening shake of his head, "and if I han't half a mind to 't!" I earnestly expressed my hope that he wouldn't, and held tighter to the tombstone on which he had put me; partly to keep myself upon it; partly, to keep myself from crying.
>
> "Now lookee here!" said the man. "Where's your mother?"
>
> "There, sir!" said I. He started, made a short run, and stopped and looked over his shoulder.
>
> From *Great Expectations* by Charles Dickens

There are several ways that Dickens adds humour to this scene. Find evidence from the text to support each one.

a Magwitch's exaggerated accent: ....

b The overuse of exclamation marks: ....

c Pip calmly reflecting on his features: ....

d Magwitch's threat to eat Pip: ....

e Pip's polite reply to the threat: ....

f Magwitch's movement: ....

2. In the following extract, a famous author recalls an encounter with a rabbit when he was a young boy playing in his garden.

> I was upside down when it happened, executing what I thought, in my childishly boyish way, to be an Olympic standard handstand when I came nose to nose with the biggest rabbit I had ever seen. His big bunny eyes met mine with a quizzical 'what on earth are you doing?' His ears were pinned back in an expression of deep thought as if he were pondering whether I was interesting or just plain ridiculous. For what seemed like a lifetime we both held the pose before he turned, playfully kicked out with both rabbity legs, and sent me tumbling to the grass. One last condescending glance and off he hopped in search of another victim.

Give five examples to show why this extract is humorous.

- ....
- ....
- ....
- ....
- ....

Making inferences

Read the following extract and explain in your own words what you learn about the character of Miss Minton from the way she is described and from the reactions of the girls. Highlight or underline the parts of the text you get your ideas from.

Remember

Making inferences involves reading between the lines to work out what is happening or what a character or relationship is like.

The girls followed Maia out into the street, but at the sight of the black-clad woman sitting stiffly in the back of the cab, her hands on her umbrella, Maia faltered. This was Miss Minton, the governess, who was going to take care of her on the journey.

"Doesn't she look fierce?" whispered Melanie.

"Poor you," mumbled Hermione.

And indeed the tall, gaunt woman looked more like a rake or a nutcracker than a human being.

The door of the cab opened. A hand in a black glove, bony and cold as a skeleton, was stretched out to help her in. Maia took it and, followed by the shrieks of her schoolmates, they set off.

From *Journey to the River Sea*
by Eva Ibbotson

....

....

....

....

....

....

....

....

The associations of language

Read the extracts below. In the first, the narrator is travelling to Corfu in a boat. In the second, the main character is travelling to Kars, in Turkey, by bus.

Decide what mood is created in each extract and identify the key words and/or phrases that help to create the mood. Write notes around the extracts if you wish.

The sea lifted smooth blue muscles of wave as it stirred in the dawn light, and the foam of our wake spread gently behind us like a white peacock's tail, glinting with bubbles. The sky was pale and stained with yellow on the eastern horizon. Ahead lay a chocolate-brown smudge of land, huddled in mist, with a frill of foam at its base. This was Corfu, and we strained our eyes to make out the exact shapes of the mountains, to discover valleys, peaks, ravines, and beaches, but it remained a silhouette. Then suddenly the sun lifted over the horizon, and the sky turned the smooth enamelled blue of a jay's eye.

From *My Family and Other Animals* by Gerald Durrell

The road signs caked with snow were impossible to read. Once the snowstorm began to rage in earnest, the driver turned off his full beam and dimmed the lights inside the bus, hoping to conjure the road out of the semi-darkness. The passengers fell into a fearful silence, with their eyes on the scene outside: the snow-covered streets of derelict villages; the dimly lit, ramshackle, one-storey houses; the roads to farther villages that were already closed; and the ravines barely visible beyond the streetlamps. If they spoke, it was in whispers.

From *Snow* by Orhan Pamuk

Spotting clichés

Below is a piece of writing which includes quite a number of clichés. These are phrases which have been used so often they have lost their impact.

Underline or highlight the clichés and then rewrite the text, replacing each cliché with something more original. You can make any other improvements you like as well.

I crept down the steps of the cellar. It was dark and I could hardly see anything at all. A shiver ran down my spine. My hand held the rail with a grip of steel. At the bottom of the stairs, I fumbled for the light switch. In the murky light I could see a battered door. I edged towards it and reached out to touch it. The door creaked open slowly. I held my breath, rooted to the spot. What was behind the door? What would I find?

....

....

....

....

....

....

....

....

....

....

....

Homonyms

Here are some sentences with homonyms. In each sentence, underline the homonym and explain what it means in this particular sentence. Then explain any other meanings of the word.

a "It's a very serious case of fraud, I'm sorry to say," said the head teacher.

....

....

b Pour the mixture carefully into the cake tin or it will spill everywhere.

....

....

c I'd like to book an appointment at the salon on Friday afternoon.

....

....

d The famous stone lies on the outskirts of the city, near the waterfall.

....

....

....

e Mrs Masood thought there might be a mouse living behind the fridge.

....

....

....

f My aunt tumbled off her bike, scraped her leg and got a ladder in her tights.

....

....

Homophones and other confusing words

This passage contains lots of words which are easily confused. Some are homophones (i.e. they sound the same). Some look similar. Choose the correct words to complete the passage.

My Mum was really angry when I got home.

"How could you lose / loose your bike?" she said. "Your / you're in big trouble. Weight / wait till your / you're father gets back. I don't know / now / no what he'll say!"

She sent me to my bedroom. I had had know /now / no tea and I was really hungry till Sam, my brother passed / past me two / to / too biscuits under the door.

I lay on my bed and wondered weather/ whether my dad would be very cross and what I could say to / too / two him. I could here / hear the other children shouting outside in are / our street. Were / we're lucky because we live in a quiet / quite rode / road so its / it's safe to play there. Then there / they're / their was the sound of a car. My dad was home!

When he stuck his head round the door, my dad was smiling.

"Come here / hear," he said. He led / lead me down stairs. I followed slowly. I wasn't sure what was happening, till I saw it. There, propped up by / bye / buy the front door was my bike!

Testing my skills

1. Why might a statement be considered controversial?

....

....

....

....

2. In what way will using humour be effective when describing a counter-argument in a persuasive text?

....

....

....

....

3. Explain the difference between implicit meaning and inference.

....

....

....

....

4. What emotions would you associate with these examples of figurative language?

   a Like a deer caught in oncoming headlights

   Emotion: ....

   b Eyes wild, fists clenched and chest thumping

   Emotion: ....

   c As a lion napping after a particularly good meal

   Emotion: ....

5. Which description best explains what a homonym is?
   Circle one answer.

   A A word that sounds the same as a word with a different meaning

   B A word that is the opposite of a given word

   C A word that can have more than one meaning

6. Which of these are homophones? Circle the correct answers.

- **A** week/weak
- **B** sour/hour
- **C** sail/sale
- **D** never/ever

7. a Write a question requiring a short answer to explain viewpoint in a text.

....

....

....

....

b Write a question requiring a short answer to explain the use of a literary technique in a text. (Hint: you can choose the literary feature.)

....

....

....

....

8. What knowledge do each of these types of short-answer question test?

a Understanding questions:

....

b Grammar questions:

....

c Vocabulary questions:

....

d Structure questions:

....

Language and literacy reference

Active voice versus passive voice – Verbs are active when the subject of the sentence (the agent) does the action. Example: *The shark swallowed the fish*. Active verbs are used more in informal speech or writing.

Verbs are passive when the subject of the sentence has the action done to it. Example: *The fish was swallowed by the shark*. Passive verbs are used in more formal writing such as reports. Examples: *An eye-witness was interviewed by the police. Results have been analysed by the sales team.*

Sometimes turning an active sentence to passive, or vice versa, simply means moving the agent:

- The shark (agent and subject) + verb = active
- The fish (object) + verb = passive

Adjective – An adjective describes a noun or adds to its meaning. They are usually found in front of a noun. Example: *Green emeralds and glittering diamonds*. Adjectives can also come after a verb. Examples: *It was big. They looked hungry*. Sometimes you can use two adjectives together. Example: *tall and handsome*. This is called an adjectival phrase.

Adjectives can be used to describe degrees of intensity. To make a comparative adjective you usually add *–er* (or use *more*). Examples: *quicker; more beautiful*. To make a superlative you add *–est* (or use *most*). Examples: *quickest; most beautiful*.

Adverb – An adverb adds further meaning to a verb. Many are formed by adding *-ly* to an adjective. Example: *slow/slowly*. They often come next to the verb in a sentence. Adverbs can tell the reader: how – *quickly, stupidly, amazingly*; where – *there, here, everywhere*; when – *yesterday, today, now*; how often – *occasionally, often*.

Adverbial phrase – The part of a sentence that tells the reader when, where or how something happens is called an adverbial phrase. It is a group of words that functions as an adverb.

Examples: *I'm going to the dentist <u>tomorrow morning</u>* (when). *The teacher spoke to us <u>as if he was in</u> a bad mood* (how); *Sam ran <u>all the way home</u>* (where). These adverbials are called adverbials of time, manner and place.

Alliteration – Alliteration occurs when two or more nearby words start with the same sound. Example: *A slow, sad, sorrowful song*.

Antecedent – An antecedent is the person or thing that a pronoun refers back to. Example: *President Alkira realised that his life was in danger*. 'President Alkira' is the antecedent here.

Antonym – An antonym is a word or phrase that means the opposite of another word or phrase in the same language. Example: *shut* is an antonym of *open*. Synonyms and antonyms can be used to add variation and depth to your writing.

Audience – The readers of a text and/or the people for whom the author is writing; the term can also apply to those who watch a film or play, or to television viewers.

Clause – A clause is a group of words that contains a subject and a verb. Example: *I ran*. In this clause, *I* is the subject and *ran* is the verb.

Cliché – An expression, idiom or phrase that has been repeated so often it has lost its significance.

Colloquial language – Informal, everyday speech as used in conversation; it may include slang expressions. It is not appropriate in written reports, essays or exams.

Colon – A colon is a punctuation mark (:) used to indicate that an example, explanation or list is being used by the writer within the sentence. Examples: *You will need: a notebook, a pencil, a notepad and a ruler. I am quick at running: as fast as a cheetah*.

Conditional tense – This tense is used to talk about something that might happen. Conditionals are sometimes called 'if' clauses. They can be used to talk about imaginary situations or possible real-life scenarios. Examples: *If it gets any colder the river will freeze. If I had a million pounds I would buy a zoo.*

Conjugate – To change the tense or subject of a verb.

Conjunction – A conjunction is a word used to link clauses within a sentence such as: *and, but, so, until, when, as.* Example: *He had a book in his hand when he stood up.*

Connectives – A connective is a word or a phrase that links clauses or sentences. Connectives can be conjunctions. Examples: *but, when, because.* Connectives can also be connecting adverbs. Examples: *then, therefore, finally.*

Continuous tense – This tense is used to tell you that something is continuing to happen. Example: *I am watching football.*

Discourse markers – Words and phrases such as *on the other hand, to sum up, however* and *therefore* are called discourse markers because they mark stages along an argument. Using them will make your paragraphs clearer and more orderly.

Exclamation – An exclamation shows someone's feelings about something. Example: *What a pity!*

Exclamation mark – An exclamation mark makes a phrase or a short sentence stand out. You usually use it in phrases like 'How silly I am!' and more freely in dialogue when people are speaking. Don't use it at the end of a long, factual sentence and don't use it too often.

Idiom – An idiom is a colourful expression which has become fixed in the language. It is a phrase which has a meaning that cannot be worked out from the meanings of the words in it. Examples: *in hot water* means 'in trouble'; *It's raining cats and dogs* means 'it's raining heavily'.

Imagery – A picture in words, often using a metaphor or simile (figurative language) which describes something in detail: writers use visual, aural (auditory) or tactile imagery to convey how something looks, sounds or feels in all forms of writing, not just fiction or poetry. Imagery helps the reader to feel like they are actually there.

Irregular verb – An irregular verb does not follow the standard grammatical rules. Each has to be learned as it does not follow any pattern. For example, *catch* becomes *caught* in the past tense, not *catched*.

Metaphor – A metaphor is a figure of speech in which one thing is actually said to be the other. Example: *This man is a lion in battle.*

Non-restrictive clause – A non-restrictive clause provides additional information about a noun. They can be taken away from the sentence and the sentence will still make sense. They are separated from the rest of the sentence by commas (or brackets). Example: *The principal, who liked order, was shocked and angry.*

Onomatopoeia – Words that imitate sounds, sensations or textures. Examples: *bang, crash, prickly, squishy.*

Paragraph – A group of sentences (minimum of two, except in modern fiction) linked by a single idea or subject. Each paragraph should contain a topic sentence. Paragraphs should be planned, linked and organised to lead up to a conclusion in most forms of writing.

Parenthetical phrase – A parenthetical phrase is a phrase that has been added into a sentence which is already complete, to provide additional information. It is usually separated from other clauses using a pair of commas, dashes or brackets (parentheses). Examples: *The leading goal scorer at the 2018 World Cup – Harry Kane, playing for England – scored six goals. The leading actor in the film, Hollywood great Gene Kelly, is captivating.*

Passive voice – See *active voice.*

Person (first, second or third) – The first person is used to talk about oneself – *I/we.* The second person is used to address the person who is listening or reading – *you*. The third person is used to refer to someone else – *he, she, it, they*.

- *I feel like I've been here for days.* (first person)
- *Look what you get when you join the club.* (second person)
- *He says it takes real courage.* (third person)

Personification – Personification can work at two levels: it can give an animal the characteristics of a human and it can give an abstract thing the characteristics of a human or an animal. Example: *I was looking Death in the face.*

Prefix – A prefix is an element placed at the beginning of a word to modify its meaning. Prefixes include: *dis-, un-, im-, in-, il-, ir-*. Examples: *impossible, inconvenient, irresponsible.*

Preposition – A preposition is a word that indicates place (*on, in*), direction (*over, beyond*) or time (*during, on*) among others.

Pronoun – A pronoun is a word that can replace a noun, often to avoid repetition. Example: *I put the book on the table. It was next to the plant. It* refers back to the book in the first sentence.

- Subject pronouns act as the subject of the sentence: *I, you, he, she, it.*
- Object pronouns act as the object of the sentence: *me, you, him, her, it, us, you, them.*
- Possessive pronouns show that something belongs to someone: *mine, yours, his, hers, its, ours, yours, theirs.*
- Demonstrative pronouns refer to things: *this, that, those, these.*

Questions – There are different types of questions.

- Closed questions – This type of question can be answered with a single-word response, can be answered with 'yes' or 'no', can be answered by choosing from a list of possible answers, and identifies a piece of specific information.

- Open questions – This type of question cannot be answered with a single-word response; it requires a more thoughtful answer than just 'yes' or 'no'.

- Leading questions – This type of question suggests what answer should be given. Example: *Why are robot servants bad for humans?* This suggests to the responder that robots are bad as the question is "why are they bad?" rather than "do you think they are bad?" Also called 'loaded questions'.

- Rhetorical questions – Rhetorical questions are questions that do not require an answer but serve to give the speaker an excuse to explain his/her views. Rhetorical questions should be avoided in formal writing and essays. Example: *Who wouldn't want to go on holiday?*

Register – The appropriate style and tone of language chosen for a specific purpose and/or audience. When speaking to your friends and family you use an informal register whereas you use a more formal tone if talking to someone older, in a position of authority or who you do not know very well. Examples: *I'm going to do up the new place.* (informal) *I am planning to decorate my new flat.* (more formal)

Regular verb – A regular verb follows the rules when conjugated (e.g. by adding *–ed* in the past tense, such as *walk* which becomes *walked*).

Relative clause – Relative clauses are a type of subordinate clause. They describe or explain something that has just been mentioned using *who, whose, which, where, whom, that* or *when*. Example: *The girl who was standing next to the counter was carrying a small dog.*

Relative pronoun – A relative pronoun does what it says – it takes an idea and relates it to a person or a thing. Be careful to use *who* for people and *which* for things. Examples: *I talked to your teacher, who told me about your unfinished homework. This is my favourite photo, which shows you the beach and the palm trees.*

Restrictive clause – Restrictive clauses identify the person or thing that is being referred to and are vital to the meaning of the sentence. They are not separated from the rest of the sentence by a comma. With restrictive clauses, you can often drop the relative pronoun. Example: *The letter [that] I wrote yesterday was lost.*

Semi-colon – A semi-colon is a punctuation mark (;) that separates two main clauses. It is stronger than a comma but not as strong as a full stop. Each clause could form a sentence by itself. Example: *I like cheese; it is delicious.*

Sentence – A sentence is a group of words that expresses a complete thought. All sentences begin with a capital letter and end with a full stop, question mark or exclamation mark.

- Simple sentences are made up of one clause. Example: *I am hungry.*

- Complex sentences are made up of one main clause and one, or more, subordinate clauses. A subordinate clause cannot stand on its own and relies on the main clause. Example: *When I joined the drama club, I did not know that it was going to be so much fun.*

- Compound sentences are made up of two or more main clauses, usually joined by a conjunction. Example: *I am hungry and I am thirsty.*

Good writers use sentences of different lengths to vary the pace of their writing. Short sentences can make a strong impact while longer sentences can make text flow.

Simile – A simile is a figure of speech in which two things are compared using the linking words *like* or *as*. Example: *In battle, he was as brave as a lion.*

Simple past tense – This tense is used to tell you that something happened in the past. Only one verb is required. Example: *I wore a hat.*

Simple present tense – This tense is used to tell you that something is happening now. Only one verb is required. Example: *I wear a hat.*

Standard English – Standard English is the form of English used in most writing and by educated speakers. It can be spoken with any accent. There are many slight differences between Standard English and local ways of speaking. Example: *We were robbed* is Standard English but in speech some people say, *We was robbed.*

Suffix – A suffix is an element placed at the end of a word to modify its meaning. Suffixes include: *-ible, -able, -ful, -less.* Examples: *useful, useless, meaningful, meaningless.*

Summary – A summary is a record of the main points of something you have read, seen or heard. Keep to the point and keep it short. Use your own words to make everything clear.

Synonym – A synonym is a word or phrase that means nearly the same as another word or phrase in the same language. Example: *shut* is a synonym of *close.* Synonyms and antonyms can be used to add variation and depth to your writing.

Syntax – The study of how words are organised in a sentence.

Tense – A tense is a verb form that shows whether events happen in the past, present or the future.

- *The Pyramids are on the west bank of the River Nile.* (present tense)

- *They were built as enormous tombs.* (past tense)

- *They will stand for centuries to come.* (future tense)

Most verbs change their spelling by adding *–ed* to form the past tense. Example: *walk/walked.* Some have irregular spellings. Example: *catch/caught.*

Topic sentence – The key sentence of a paragraph that contains the principal idea or subject being discussed.

Word and definition

Notes

abdomen *noun*
the lower front part of a person's or animal's body, containing the digestive organs; the belly

addictive *adjective*
cannot be given up

adjacent *adjective*
near by or next to

admittedly *adverb*
as an agreed fact; without denying it

advocate *verb*
to speak on behalf of others

aeon *noun*
an indefinite and very long period of time

allow *verb*
to let someone do something

arouse *verb*
to stir up a feeling in someone

arrowy *adjective*
shaped like an arrow

aspect *noun*
one part of a problem or situation

bandwagon unjumped *noun + adjective*
from the saying 'to jump on the bandwagon' meaning to join other people in doing something successful

bedspread *noun*
a covering spread over a bed

boundless *adjective*
without limits

burst *verb*
to break open suddenly and with force

chainmail *noun*
flexible armour consisting of small metal rings linked together

challenge *noun*
a new and exciting but difficult task or activity

char *verb*
to make something black or become black by burning

charge, to be in *verb*
to have responsibility or control

Word and definition	**Notes**

charisma *noun*
the special quality that makes a person attractive or influential

charnel *noun*
a building or vault in which corpses or bones are piled

chunky *adjective*
large; broad; thick

clueless *adjective*
having no knowledge, understanding or ability

collide *verb*
to crash into something

comfortable *adjective*
cosy

conjecture *verb*
to guess

cool *adjective*
calm, not enthusiastic

cortical *adjective*
to do with the outer grey material forming part of the brain

countless *adjective*
too many to count

crack *verb*
1 to break or split with a crack; 2 to succeed with something (colloquial)

critical *adjective*
1 pointing out faults or weaknesses in a person or thing; 2 to do with the assessment of a literary or artistic work; 3 to do with or at a crisis, very serious

dangerous *adjective*
likely to kill or harm

delightful *adjective*
giving pleasure

desolation *noun*
1 lonely and sad state; 2 uninhabited or barren place

devious *adjective*
underhand and cunning

dishevelled *adjective*
ruffled and untidy in appearance

dismantle *verb*
to take something to pieces

ditch *verb*
discard; get rid of

Word and definition	Notes

douse *verb*
to pour water over something

enter *verb*
1 to go in; **2** to register as a competitor

epic *adjective*
on a grand or heroic scale, like an epic

epic *noun*
a long, usually ancient poem about the deeds and adventures of heroic or legendary figures or the past history of a nation

essentially *adverb*
1 vitally, crucially; **2** basically, in essence

eternity *noun*
1 everlasting time; **2** a very long time

execute *verb*
1 to put someone to death as punishment; **2** to perform an action or manoeuvre

explode *verb*
burst or suddenly release energy with a loud noise

exquisite *adjective*
very beautiful or delicate

famous *adjective*
known to very many people

femininazies *noun*
people who have strong views about gender issues (colloquial)

forage *verb*
to go searching for something, especially food or fuel

foray *noun*
a sudden attack or raid

frankly *adverb*
in a way that makes thoughts and feelings clear to people; candidly

furnace *noun*
a type of large oven that produces great heat, especially for melting metals or making glass

ghastly *adjective*
very unpleasant or bad

handy *adjective*
1 useful; **2** good at doing something

haul *noun*
an amount or number of things taken or obtained by effort

Word and definition

hefty *adjective*
large and strong
herder *noun*
a person who looks after a herd of animals
historic *adjective*
important or famous in history
horsemanship *noun*
skilled riding of a horse
hostile *adjective*
1 unfriendly and aggressive; **2** opposed to something
hustle *verb*
1 to hurry; **2** push or shove rudely
idiocy *noun*
stupid behaviour
impact *verb*
to have an effect on
improbable *adjective*
unlikely
improvise *verb*
to make something with whatever is available
inert *adjective*
not moving or reacting
influential *adjective*
having great influence
inhabited *adjective*
lived in
inhospitable *adjective*
giving no shelter or good weather
inviting *adjective*
attractive or tempting
jeopardy *noun*
danger of harm or failure
jittery *adjective*
nervous or unable to relax
lefties *noun*
people with socialist or 'left wing' political views (colloquial)
ligature *noun*
a thing used in tying something, especially in surgical operations
magnificent *adjective*
splendid, beautiful, impressive

Notes

Word and definition

mass *noun*
in science, the quantity of physical matter that a thing contains
meander *verb*
to take a winding course; to wander
melancholy *adjective*
sad; gloomy
miserably *adverb*
in a pitiable manner; terribly
monarch *noun*
a king, queen, emperor or empress ruling a country
mortify *verb*
to humiliate someone or make them feel very ashamed
multi-million-selling *adjective*
having sold many millions of copies
murky *adjective*
dark and gloomy
new *adjective*
not existing before; just made, invented, discovered or received
nomadic *adjective*
of a lifestyle based on moving home to find pasture for animals
observe *verb*
to see and notice someone or something; to watch carefully
palatable *adjective*
edible and pleasant to eat
paradisiacal *adjective*
ideal and idyllic
parched *adjective*
very dry or thirsty
penitentiary *noun*
a prison for people convicted of serious crimes
perceive *noun*
to see, notice or understand something
perplex *verb*
to bewilder or puzzle somebody
plant *verb*
to put something where it will grow
plausible *adjective*
seeming to be honest or worth believing but perhaps deceptive
pliable *adjective*
1 easy to bend, flexible; 2 easy to influence or control

Notes

Word and definition

Notes

plough *verb*
to cut a path across somewhere, with effort or difficulty

portray *verb*
to show or describe a person in a particular way

posture *noun*
a particular position of the body or the way in which a person stands, sits or walks

predictably *adverb*
always in the same way; showing no imagination

process *verb*
to put something through a manufacturing or other process

prone *adjective*
likely to do something or be affected by it

queasy *adjective*
feeling slightly sick

radiant *adjective*
radiating heat, light, brightness or an emotion

radiate *verb*
to send out light, heat, etc.

ravener *noun*
1 a bird of prey; **2** someone who preys or plunders

receive *verb*
to accept something from someone else

reins (of power) *noun*
control of a country

remote *adjective*
1 far away in place or time; **2** isolated or inaccessible

renowned *adjective*
famous or celebrated

retiring *adjective*
shy; avoiding company

reusable *adjective*
can be used again

rigorous *adjective*
thorough and strict

rip *verb*
to tear across something roughly

Word and definition	Notes

rumour *noun*
information that spreads to a lot of people but may not be true

saw-pit *noun*
a pit over which timber is positioned to be sawn

scrape *verb*
to pass something hard across the surface of something else to clean, smooth or damage it

scrubland *noun*
land covered with low trees and bushes

scummy *adjective*
having froth or dirt on top (usually on a liquid)

serrated *adjective*
having a notched edge

shrill *adjective*
sounding very high and piercing

smoulder *verb*
to burn slowly without a flame

sonata *noun*
a piece of music for one instrument or two, in several movements

sound *verb*
1 to produce a noise; 2 to give an impression when heard

spatial *adjective*
to do with space

stunning *adjective*
extremely beautiful or attractive

suitor *noun*
a man who is courting a woman

superficial *adjective*
1 on the surface; 2 not deep or thorough

theorise *verb*
to form a theory or theories

tier *noun*
each of a series of rows or levels placed one above the other

torrential *adjective*
pouring down violently

travel *verb*
to journey across long distances

understandably *adverb*
1 in a way that can be understood; 2 reasonablly or naturally

undoubtedly *adverb*
certainly; without any doubt

Word and definition

ungainly *adjective*
awkward or clumsy in appearance or movement

unjumped *adjective*
(made up word) not taken advantage of

unrivalled *adjective*
unequalled

vermin *noun*
animals or insects that damage crops or food or carry disease, such as rats and fleas

window-sill *noun*
a ledge or sill forming the bottom part of a window

wonderful *adjective*
marvellous or excellent

Notes

....

....

....

....

....

....